For Jacob

DAN TOOMBS

# THE CURRY GUY

# AIR FRYER

## 50 Simple Curry Favourites

Photography by Kris Kirkham

Quadrille

# CONTENTS

Preface 6
Let's Get Started 8

## STARTERS AND SNACKS 12

Poppadums with Onion Chutney 14
Aloo Tikki Chaat 17
Onion Bhajis with Pakora Sauce 18
Chicken 65 20
Lamb Seekh Kebabs 23
Quick Tandoori Chicken Legs 24
Lahori Fish Tikka 26
Beef Chapli Kebabs 28
Paneer Papad Rolls 30
Hariyali Paneer Tikka and Vegetable Skewers 33
Nargisi Koftas 34

## CURRIES 36

Air Fryer Base Sauce 38
Chicken Tikka Masala 40
Chicken Korma 42
Chicken Jalfrezi 45
Chicken Chasni 47
Chicken Rezala 48
Chicken Chilli Garlic 51
Chicken Pathia 52
Chicken Ceylon 55
Chicken Pasanda 56
Chicken Methi 59
Chicken Dhansak 61
Chicken Chaat 62
Chicken Biryani 64
Lamb Dopiaza 67
Lamb Rogan Josh 69
Lamb Achari 70
Keema 72
Beef Bhuna 75
Lamb Andrak 77

Lamb Madras 78
Saag Paneer 80
Butter Paneer 83
Aloo Gobi 85
Rajma 86

## TANDOORI FAVOURITES 88

Chicken Tikka 90
Meat Tikka with Cucumber Raita 93
Easy Whole Tandoori Chicken 94
Southern Style Tandoori Chicken 97
Tandoori Lamb Chops with Coriander Chutney 99
Cheese Filled Kofta with Chilli Raita 101
Tandoori Prawns 103
Tandoori Sea Bream 104
Stuffed Mushrooms 106

## BASICS AND SIDE DISHES 108

Perfect Air Fryer Basmati Rice 110
Fried Pilau Rice 111
Masala Fries 112
Bombay Potatoes 114
Instant Naans 117
Spice Blends 118
Garlic Ginger and Chilli Paste 120
Fried Onions 120
Easy Tamarind Chutney 121
Coriander, Mint and Mango Chutney 121
Tarka Dal 122

Index 123
Acknowledgements 126

# PREFACE

You have in your hands a cookbook I never thought I'd write but I'm so happy I was given the opportunity to do so. Air fryers are like mini tandoor ovens but are less expensive to purchase and run, and they heat up so much faster. In the following pages you will learn to prepare recipes that I have spent the past year developing. Many of the recipes may not be what you would normally associate with air fryer cooking, but they work! Welcome to my world of air frying, where deliciousness meets convenience. Air frying curries is not a replacement for more traditional cooking methods (I will never stop cooking curries in a hot pan!). But it is a convenient, money-saving and fun way to cook up a great meal.

I think it's fair to say that many people who have purchased an air fryer over the past few year, did so because air fryers offer a healthier alternative to shallow- and deep-fat frying. While that's true, there is so much more that you can do with these small, eco-friendly, economical and efficient ovens. In this book you will find not only the most popular fried, grilled and roasted Indian takeaway dishes but also learn how to prepare your favourite curries and side dishes.

Every method of cooking has its limitations. You might think that there are some things that just can't be cooked in an air fryer, but I have spent hundreds of hours experimenting to get these recipes just right for you. I looked for the obvious limitations that come with air frying and have worked out ways to get around them.

So before you jump in and start cooking up that restaurant-style chicken madras or tarka dal, be sure to not only read my instructions but use your eyes too. Air fryers heat up quickly, unlike conventional ovens, so you can and should check what you are cooking and react accordingly.

My metal air fryer dish might have a thicker base than yours, for example. Air fryers, like ovens, vary too. You will want to check what you are cooking and stir or reduce/increase the cooking heat if you feel you need to. Pay attention to what you are cooking, take notes if necessary and you will enjoy some amazing air fried food.

Personally, I like to think of air fryers as what they are: fantastic small ovens, and not just as an alternative machine for frying more healthily. In fact, in some of the recipes more oil or ghee is called for than needed so that you can prepare a dish just as you would expect it to be served at your local takeaway. You can, of course, use less oil if you like.

Whether you're a busy parent wanting a quick and convenient meal solution, a student looking for inexpensive ways to quickly cook up your favourite takeaway meal or a health-conscious cook looking for lighter alternatives to your favourite fried foods, *The Curry Guy Air Fryer* will show you the way!

So, dust off your air fryer, gather your ingredients and get ready to go on a culinary adventure like no other. From delicious seekh kebabs, onion bhajis and tikka aloo to mouthwatering chicken tikka masala, jalfrezi and chasni curries, you will find them all here. Not only that, you will be able to enjoy them with air fried rice, naans and poppadums. Is air fried rice even possible?! I can assure you it is. Let's fire up those air fryers and get cooking!

I hope you enjoy cooking and trying this new collection of air fryer recipes as much as I enjoyed developing them. If you have any questions about any of the recipes, please get in touch. I manage all of my own social media accounts, so if you ask a question, it will be me who answers. I'm @TheCurryGuy on X, Facebook, TikTok and Instagram and would love to hear from you.

# LET'S GET STARTED

Here are a few badges that will help you find the recipes you want to try.

**Gluten-free:** If you are on a gluten-free diet, then you probably already know to look for hidden gluten in common ingredients. Just in case you don't, this badge will help you find the recipes that are gluten-free or can easily be made so by using gluten-free options.

**Vegetarian:** When you see this badge, the recipe is vegetarian. If you are vegetarian, don't just skip past the non-veg curries though. They can all be made vegetarian using paneer, air fried potatoes and/or roasted vegetables. Just leave out the meat and add what you want to the sauce.

**Quick:** Look for this badge if you want to whip up a meal in minutes with little fuss.

**Marinating and Soaking:** This badge indicates ingredients need to be soaked in water before cooking and/or will benefit from a longer marinating time.

**Special Equipment Needed:** When you see this badge, you will know that a cooking accessory will either help with the cook or is essential to cooking. Things such as metal or silicone air fryer dishes, foil and wooden skewers will either be required or helpful.

## HOW TO USE THESE RECIPES

All of the recipes should be used as guides as we don't all have the same air fryers nor taste preferences. The great thing about air fryers is that they heat up quickly, so you can regularly check the progress of the meal you are cooking. The following tips will help you get each recipe just right.

When it comes to flavour, I don't want to have anyone writing to me to say the Madras wasn't hot enough or the Vindaloo was too spicy! Taste as you go. You can easily do that when cooking in an air fryer. Get to know your spices and add more of those you like and less of those you don't.

### GETTING TO KNOW YOUR AIR FRYER

Air fryers are manufactured in different sizes, and suit most budgets and cooking requirements. Many have pre-set functions and modes like baking, dehydration – even rotisserie. Then there are multi-cookers, which, in addition to air frying, offer functions like searing, baking, proving, slow cooking and pressure cooking. I have kept the recipes in this book simple so that they will work for all kinds of air fryers, but you can and should experiment with the different cooking modes available to you.

Air fryers do vary. Some are small and budget-friendly. Some have two or more cooking chambers, which can be a real time saver. Some premium air fryers come with higher wattage for faster cooking. No matter which air fryer you have, these recipes will all work. That said, you might want to tweak the recipes depending on your appliance.

It's worth noting that just because the instructions for a recipe say to air fry at 200°C/400°F, you don't have to do exactly that! I have tried and tested these recipes to give you a good place to start, but if your air fryer has other functions you would like to experiment with at different temperatures, go for it. Feel free to get adventurous. Have fun testing out different cooking modes, if you have them. For example, if yours is a multi-cooker that also sears, you could use that instead of air frying. The possibilities are many and it's all in your hands.

If you have been air frying for a while, you will know that you can always open the drawer to check on what you are cooking. If you are new to air frying, this is what's so great about it. Once the drawer has been closed, the cooking temperature goes right back up, almost immediately!

**Note:** Throughout this book, the 'drawer' refers to the part of the air fryer you cook in, whether that's a pull-out chamber or the main compartment of a multi-cooker or oven-style air fryer. The 'basket' is the removable metal insert.

## USING OIL TO COOK

You might be one of the millions who use an air fryer to cut back on your oil intake. These recipes can all be prepared with oil spray so no worries there. Many people, however, are now air frying because it's an economical, convenient and less messy way of cooking. If that's you, I have you covered too!

All of the recipes were developed to achieve optimum flavour. Sometimes that means infusing whole spices, aromatic ingredients and often ground spices and herbs into a couple of tablespoons of oil. Not only does this add flavour to a curry but the oil also helps speed up the cooking process. You don't have to do that though.

## ALTERNATIVES TO TEMPERING IN OIL

I have tried to make these recipes taste just like they were cooked in a hot pan on the hob (stove), and I can assure you they do. I use my air fryer not as a healthy way of cooking but as an alternative way of cooking a good curry or side dish.

If you are on a reduced-calorie diet, you can still get a lot of the flavour without tempering whole spices and other aromatics in oil. For example, if a recipe calls for tempering a cinnamon stick and cardamom pods in oil before adding the sauce ingredients to the pan, you could just add a pinch of ground cinnamon and cardamom to the sauce to taste.

Aromatic ingredients such as curry leaves, cassia leaves, ginger, etc. all air fry really well coated with oil spray. Doing this, you might need to get creative and air fry curry leaves and other aromatic ingredients when you air fry the sauce base. You can, of course, remove these ingredients before blending the sauce if you want to add them whole to finish the recipe.

## CAN YOU SCALE UP THE CURRY RECIPES TO SERVE MORE?

I developed these curry recipes to serve 1–2 people as this is the perfect amount for most air fryers and is also the standard serving size at curry houses. In my air fryer, the cake tin I use is no more than half-full when I cook the recipes, and this is best. Any fuller and you could have steam or splatter issues when you cook the curries. It takes at least 10 minutes for the sauce to heat up so, contrary to popular belief, spitting and steam is not an issue when you air fry in these smaller portion sizes.

Unless you have a really large air fryer, I don't recommend scaling up the recipes. They will take longer to cook, and steam and splatter might be an issue.

On the topic of steam and splatter, I have not had this problem with any of the curries in any of the air fryers I tested. In fact, you will get more steam from a whole chicken than you will a curry. No worries there!

**Which pans?** You will need metal pans that fit inside your cooking area (the drawer). I use an air fryer cake barrel tin that is a common accessory for air fryers. Mine is 18cm (7in) in diameter but you will want to measure your drawer to ensure you purchase the right size for your model. Do not opt for silicone air fryer inserts when cooking curries as they do not get hot enough.

**Alternative to using a pan:** In many air fryers, you can simply remove the rack and cook a curry in the drawer itself. I prefer using pans as they are easier to clean and can also be used to serve the curry.

**Cooking times:** The cooking times refer to total cooking time, and assume you are using an air fryer with one drawer. These times can usually be reduced if you are cooking different elements of the recipe simultaneously. For example, cook your tandoori chicken in one basket and your onions and bell pepper in the other.

With regard to the curries, there is another thing that will speed up cooking. Those curries that call for tempering spices will cook a couple of minutes faster than those that don't because of the hot oil. If you like, you could heat 2 tablespoons of oil in your pan before adding the sauce, even if the recipe doesn't call for it. This will not only cook the curry faster but will give you a nice sheen on the surface, similar to that you might expect at a curry house.

**Cooking heat:** I have developed each of these recipes to be air fried no higher than 200°C (400°F). I did this because many air fryers only have a single air fryer function and 200°C (400°F) is their maximum cooking heat. This temperature works fine for all of the recipes. If your model has other functions, such as Max Crisp, Bake and Prove, there is no reason why you shouldn't try them with the recipes. Keep an eye on everything as it cooks and you really can't go wrong.

That's just one of the great things about cooking recipes like these in an air fryer. You can open the air fryer whenever you like to check what you're cooking. When you close the drawer again, your air fryer will almost instantly go back to the set temperature.

## USEFUL EQUIPMENT

- **Chef's knife** – One good chef's knife is all you need. Many people purchase a whole set of knives but I recommend purchasing just one good-quality, sharp chef's knife that you are comfortable using.

- **Kettle** – Many of the recipes call for stock, either homemade or from stock (bouillon) cubes. If using stock cubes, it is best to make the stock right before using it so that it is warm or mildly hot. Using warm or hot stock will speed up the air fryer cooking process.

- **Stick blender** – Depending on the mixing bowl you are using, you might find a stick blender comes in handy for blending the curry sauces until smooth. Personally, I find a blender better for doing this.

- **Blender** – A good blender will always come in handy. You can add the ingredients for the sauces directly to the blender and then blend until smooth.

- **Meat thermometer** – Get yourself a meat thermometer if you don't already have one. They come in a range of prices but they all do the same job. Having a good meat thermometer eliminates the need to cut into meat to guesstimate when it is properly cooked through.

- **Metal spice dabba** – This is not only great for storing spices: remove the spices and use this metal pan with its tight-fitting lid to cook a biryani or rice.

- **Metal air fryer cake tin inserts** – I recommend purchasing a small cake tin or two that fit into your air fryer. Cake tins are commonly used to cook stews and curries and other things in air fryers. In some air fryers, you can simply add food directly to the air fryer. That's fine too, but I find that using cake tins or other small metal pans helps cook the food faster, and they are a lot easier to clean afterwards.

# STARTERS AND SNACKS

The following starters and snacks are all hugely popular in Indian restaurants. Some of these recipes are accompanied by an optional raita or chutney. These dips are not calculated into the preparation and cooking time but can usually be whipped up while the air fryer is working its magic.

The chutneys and raitas are all delicious served with different dishes and can be mixed and matched to other recipes. So, if you like the look of the onion chutney that is served with the poppadums on page 14 but you want to serve it with onion bhajis instead of pakora sauce, then go for it!

# POPPADUMS WITH ONION CHUTNEY

SERVES 2–4

Cooking poppadums in an air fryer is easy and you really can get excellent results without the mess of deep-fat frying. Of course, poppadums can also be cooked in a microwave or conventional oven but the way the hot air flows in an air fryer means you get superior results. If you happen to have an air fryer with two cooking chambers, you can cook your poppadums and a good curry to go with them at the same time.

PREP TIME: 1 MIN
COOKING TIME: 24 MINS

4 or more papads
2 tbsp rapeseed (canola) oil, for brushing, or oil spray

FOR THE ONION CHUTNEY
1 large red onion, finely chopped
1 tbsp lemon juice, or to taste
2 green finger chillies, finely chopped
3 tbsp finely chopped coriander (cilantro)
2 tsp mint sauce (I use Colman's but any will do)
½ tsp Kashmiri chilli powder
½ tsp nigella seeds
2 level tbsp ketchup (I use Heinz)
2 tsp smooth mango chutney
¼ tsp red food colouring powder (optional for colour)
Salt, to taste

Papads are really light and tend to fly around in the air fryer basket as the heat flows. To stop this from happening, preheat your air fryer to 200°C (400°F) and then lightly brush or spray the papad on both sides with oil. Place it under the basket. Problem solved! Forget to do that and your papad will get sucked up into the element and will burn.

Cook the papad in this way for 4 minutes and then remove the basket and turn it over. Return the basket and cook for another 4–6 minutes. Remove your cooked poppadum and let it rest for a couple of minutes. When you first take it out of the air fryer, it won't be very crispy but it will crisp up as it rests. Repeat with the remaining papads.

TO MAKE THE CHUTNEY

This first step is optional but will get you really cold and crispy onions. Place the chopped red onion in a bowl of ice-cold water with a squeeze of lemon juice for 10 minutes. Strain and shake off the excess water and return the chopped onion to the bowl.

Add the green chillies, coriander (cilantro), mint sauce, chilli powder, nigella seeds, ketchup and smooth mango chutney and stir well to combine. You want the onion to be completely coated with the other ingredients.

Add salt and lemon juice to taste, and if you prefer a red glow like you find at many curry houses, add the red food colouring powder. Food colouring adds no flavour so you would only add it for presentation reasons. Stir well to combine it all and place in your fridge for about 30 minutes or serve immediately with your poppadums.

# ALOO TIKKI CHAAT
SERVES 4

These aloo tikki are delicious served simply, with ketchup for dipping. Here, I give a few optional extras so that you can make them into the famous street food snack, aloo tikki chaat, if you like. The recipe calls for mashed potatoes – the quickest method is to boil cubed potatoes in water and mash them when soft. If you want to make this all in your air fryer, you can do that by following the instructions below.

**PREP TIME: 15 MINS**
**COOKING TIME: 35 MINS**
**(USING BOILED**
**MASH METHOD)**

3 medium potatoes, boiled, then mashed (optional, see intro)
1 medium red onion, finely chopped
2–3 green finger chillies
3 tbsp finely chopped coriander (cilantro)
1½ tbsp garlic and ginger paste
½ tsp ground turmeric
½ tsp ground cumin
½ tsp freshly ground black pepper
1 tsp ground coriander
2 tsp cornflour (cornstarch) or rice flour
2 tbsp rapeseed (canola) oil or oil spray
Salt, to taste

**FOR THE CHAAT**
**(OPTIONAL)**
5 tbsp shop-bought tamarind sauce or Easy tamarind chutney (see page 121)
5 tbsp Chilli raita (see page 101)
5 tbsp Coriander, mint and mango chutney (see page 120)
5 tbsp fine/nylon sev

If not boiling the potatoes, preheat your air fryer to 200°C (400°F). Place the unpeeled potatoes in the air fryer basket and cook about 50 minutes, turning halfway through cooking. The cooking time will vary depending on the size of your potatoes. They are ready for mashing when you can stick a fork in with little to no resistance. Peel the potatoes and mash them in a mixing bowl.

Add the remaining ingredients up to and including 1 tablespoon of the oil, or spray the mixture with a little oil spray. Mix well to combine completely. Wet your hands with a little water and form the potato mixture into 8–10 equal patties.

Now spray the air fryer basket with oil and place them inside. Set the air fryer to 200°C (400°F) and air fry for 15 minutes, turning the patties once and basting from time to time with the remaining oil or oil spray. When heated through, golden brown and crispy on the exterior, your tikki are ready to serve.

To serve as aloo tikki chaat, place the hot aloo tikki on a serving plate and top with one or more of the sauces. I usually do this with squeezy bottles for better presentation and then top with the sev.

**NOTE**
Fine/nylon sev is a crunchy topping made from gram (chickpea) flour and it is available online and at specialty grocers. It is a nice and popular addition to aloo tikki chaat but it's not essential. For added texture and flavour, you might also like to top your aloo tikki chaat with finely chopped red onion.

# ONION BHAJIS WITH PAKORA SAUCE

SERVES 4

**Who doesn't love onion bhajis to start off a meal? These air fryer onion bhajis are better than many deep-fried versions I have had at restaurants. The key to getting this recipe right is to be very careful when adding the flours. Many chefs add too much flour, which results in stodgy bhajis and you don't want that. Once cooked, bring it all together with the delicious but optional pakora sauce.**

PREP TIME: 15 MINS,
    PLUS SITTING TIME
COOKING TIME: 15 MINS

2 white onions, slightly larger than tennis balls
1 red onion, slightly larger than a tennis ball
1 tsp fine sea salt
1½ tbsp Garlic, ginger and chilli paste (see page 120)
2.5cm (1in) piece of ginger, peeled and julienned
2 tbsp curry leaves, roughly chopped
1 tsp Kashmiri chilli powder (more or less to taste)
2 tbsp rapeseed (canola) oil or oil spray
½ tsp ground turmeric
4 tbsp rice flour
Approx. 140g (5oz) gram flour, sifted
3 tbsp finely chopped coriander (cilantro)

FOR THE PAKORA SAUCE
1 onion, finely chopped
2 tbsp smooth mango chutney
3 tbsp ketchup
1 tsp mint sauce
200ml (1 cup) natural yoghurt
½ tsp roasted cumin seeds
½ tsp Kashmiri chilli powder, or to taste
1 tbsp sugar, or to taste
1 tsp lemon juice, or to taste
½ tsp red food colouring powder (optional)
Milk (optional)
Salt, to taste

Peel and cut the onions in half and then finely slice them. Mix the salt into them in a mixing bowl and set aside for 1 hour or up to 4 hours.

After 1 hour, the onions will be limp and moist. Squeeze the onions to release the excess water into the bowl. Add the remaining ingredients, being careful not to add too much gram flour. You should easily be able to pick up some of the onion mixture and form it into a ball and you should see more onion than dough. So only add enough flour to be able to do this.

Divide the mixture into small round or sloppy bhajis. Heat your air fryer to 200°C (400°F). Spray the basket generously with oil. Place the bhajis in the basket. You may need to cook these in batches, depending on the size of your cooking chamber.

Air fry for 15 minutes, turning once, until your onion bhajis are crispy and ready to serve. Cook a little longer if not. Serve hot or at room temperature. They are best hot from the air fryer.

FOR THE PAKORA SAUCE

Whisk all of the ingredients together, except for the food colouring, milk and salt.

Once the sauce is nicely combined, add the food colouring, if using. If the sauce is too thick for your liking, stir in a little milk until you are happy with the consistency. Season with salt to taste before serving.

# CHICKEN 65
SERVES 4

**Chicken 65 is a famous stir-fried dish. Traditionally, the chicken pieces are deep-fried in a batter before being stir-fried in a little oil with the other ingredients. This recipe gets great results and you probably won't be able to tell the difference between it and the full-fat version. Cleaning up will be a lot quicker and easier too!**

PREP TIME: 15 MINS,
  PLUS MARINATING
  (OPTIONAL)
COOKING TIME: 20 MINS

500g (1lb 2oz) skinless chicken
  breasts or thighs, cut into
  5cm (2in) pieces
Oil spray
1–2 tbsp rapeseed (canola) oil
½ tsp black mustard seeds
½ tsp cumin seeds
20 fresh or frozen curry leaves
2 green finger chillies, sliced in
  half lengthwise
6 garlic cloves, finely chopped
5cm (2in) piece of ginger,
  peeled and julienned
2 spring onions (scallions),
  roughly chopped
1–2 tbsp hot sauce (I use
  Frank's), plus extra to serve
1 tbsp lemon juice
Salt, to taste

FOR THE SPICED BATTER

1 egg white
1 tbsp garlic and ginger paste
½ tsp ground turmeric
2 tsp ground cumin
2 tsp ground coriander
1 tsp chilli powder
2 tsp tandoori masala
½ tsp salt
1 tsp freshly ground
  black pepper
2 tbsp cornflour (cornstarch)
2 tbsp rice flour

Place the chicken in a bowl and add the egg white, garlic and ginger paste, turmeric, cumin, coriander, chilli powder, tandoori masala, salt and pepper. Mix well to combine so that the chicken is completely coated with the spice mixture. Allow to marinate for 30 minutes or up to 24 hours. If you're in a rush, you could go straight to cooking but longer marination time does have its flavour benefits.

Place the marinated chicken in a large bag, such as a freezer bag, and add the flours. Seal and shake to coat the chicken with the flours.

Preheat the air fryer to 200˚C (400˚F) and spray the basket with cooking oil spray. Shake off any excess flour from the chicken and place the chicken in one layer in the basket. Spray generously with oil and air fry for 10 minutes, turning once halfway through cooking. Transfer to a plate and set aside.

Now place a cake tin or another suitable metal pan that fits into your air fryer and add the oil, using 2 tablespoons of oil if you want your chicken 65 to be closer to the traditional version. Allow the oil to heat up for 4 minutes and then add the mustard seeds and let them fry for a minute. Then stir in the cumin seeds, chillies and curry leaves and let them infuse their flavour into the oil for another minute.

Stir in the garlic, ginger and half of the spring onions (scallions) and fry for another minute or two to soften, but be careful not to burn the garlic. Add the fried chicken and give it all a good stir to coat the chicken. Stir in your hot sauce of choice to coat. Air fry for another 2 minutes or until the chicken is heated through and crispy. Add the remaining spring onions (scallions) and stir to warm them through. They should still be fresh and crispy in texture, unlike the other spring onions, which will be cooked through. Pour the lemon juice all over it and season with salt to taste. Serve immediately.

# LAMB SEEKH KEBABS
SERVES 2–4

**This is a simplified version of my grilled lamb seekh kebabs that I normally squeeze onto metal skewers and cook over fire. You'll still get the amazing flavour, but as these are cooked in the air fryer basket, you don't have to knead the meat for as long, unless you want to. You can use any minced (ground) meat for this recipe but, personally, I prefer lamb or mutton.**

PREP TIME: 10 MINS
COOKING TIME: 8 MINS

500g (1lb 2oz) minced (ground) lamb (80:20 meat to fat ratio)
½ red onion, very finely chopped
1 tbsp Garlic, ginger and chilli paste (see page 120)
1 tbsp finely chopped mint leaves
1 tbsp finely chopped coriander (cilantro)
½ tsp salt
2 tsp Kashmiri chilli powder (more or less to taste)
1 tsp ground coriander
½ tsp ground cumin
½ tsp freshly ground black pepper
Oil spray

TO FINISH

1 tbsp melted ghee or butter (optional)
¼ English cucumber, peeled, seeded and grated or finely diced
½ red onion, thinly sliced
1 lemon, quartered
Flaky salt, to taste
Chilli raita (see page 101), to serve

Place all the kebab ingredients in a mixing bowl and knead with your hands for 3–5 minutes to mix well and break the meat down until fine and smooth. You can start cooking immediately or let the meat mixture marinate in the fridge overnight. If you would like a smoky flavour, as if the meat was cooked over fire, try the dhungar method described on page 89.

When ready to cook, preheat your air fryer to 200°C (400°F). Divide the meat mixture into four equal balls and then roll them out into sausage shapes. Spray the cooking basket and kebabs with oil and place them inside to air fry for 10 minutes, turning once halfway through cooking.

After 10 minutes, the meat will be cooked. You can decide to remove the kebabs and serve, or char them for a couple of minutes longer. Transfer to a serving plate and season with flaky salt to taste. Drizzle with the melted ghee, if using, and serve garnished with the cucumber, red onion and lemon wedges, with chilli raita or your choice of sauce on the side.

PRESENTATION TIP

Soak four wooden skewers in water for 30 minutes. Take a plastic freezer bag and cut it open down the sides, leaving the bottom seam intact. Lay it flat on a clean work surface so that the bottom seam is in the middle and spray it all over with oil to coat. Take one of the meatballs and stick one of the skewers down the centre. Place it where the bottom seam of the bag is and fold the plastic over it. It should look like a freezer bag again with the meatball and skewer where the bottom of the bag is.

Take hold of the bag that is on the work surface. Then take a long chef's knife and press the back of the knife up against the meatball, horizontally to the skewer. Press down and begin pushing the meatball with the knife. As you do this, the top flap of the bag will go along with the movement and the meat will start rolling down the skewer into a perfect sausage shape, like you find when you purchase kebab skewers at the supermarket. Repeat with the remaining skewers and meat.

# QUICK TANDOORI CHICKEN LEGS

SERVES 2–4

**By quick tandoori chicken legs, I mean that they are very quick to cook in your air fryer. This recipe will benefit if you allow the chicken to marinate for at least 30 minutes or overnight. That said, if you're in a rush for this curry-house classic, just go straight to cooking. For a delicious smoky flavour, be sure to use the Dhungar method on page 89.**

PREP TIME: 10 MINS,
  PLUS MARINATING
  (OPTIONAL)
COOKING TIME: 20 MINS

4 large chicken legs with
  thighs, skin removed
Juice of 2 lemons
1 tsp rapeseed (canola) oil
2 tbsp Garlic, ginger and
  chilli paste (see page 120)
½ tsp red food colouring
  powder (optional)
120ml (½ cup) Greek yoghurt
1–2 tbsp Kashmiri chilli
  powder (more or less to
  taste)
1 tbsp ground cumin
1 tbsp ground coriander
1 tsp garam masala
2 tsp freshly ground
  black pepper
1 tsp salt, plus extra to serve
Oil spray
Lemon or lime wedges, to
  serve

Score the chicken legs in several places on both sides and place in a mixing bowl. Add the lemon juice, oil, garlic, ginger and chilli paste and, if you want your chicken legs to be bright red, add the food colouring. The container of the red food colouring powder you purchase will most likely state not to apply directly to food. That's how it's done at restaurants though, so I'll let you decide. Set aside.

Whisk the yoghurt and all the remaining ingredients together until smooth. Pour this over the chicken and rub it right into the flesh. Allow to marinate for 30 minutes and up to 24 hours for optimum flavour, or go straight to cooking.

Preheat the air fryer to 200°C (400°F). Lightly spray your cooking basket with oil and then place the chicken in the basket. If you have an air fryer with two cooking chambers, you can cook it all at once. If not, you might need to cook in batches. Just wrap the first batch with foil to keep it warm and then cook the second batch.

Place the chicken in your air fryer and air fry for 18–20 minutes, turning at the halfway point. The chicken is ready when the juices run clear when pricked with a knife, or you could and should play it safe by using a meat thermometer. Chicken is cooked when it reaches an internal temperature of 74°C/165°F.

Serve with lemon or lime wedges and a little flaky salt to taste – you can add this at the table.

# LAHORI FISH TIKKA
SERVES 2

The marinade for this recipe works well with any meaty white fish. I have also tried it with mackerel and salmon in the air fryer with great results. Sometimes I use this recipe with a selection of different fish, both on and off the bone, which makes a delicious fish platter for a main meal. In this recipe, you use fish tikka or boneless fish cut into bite-sized pieces. The fish can be served as a starter or you could add the air fried fish to a curry at the end of cooking and heat it through in the sauce. Not too long though or it will fall apart.

PREP TIME: 10 MINS,
PLUS MARINATING
(OPTIONAL)
COOKING TIME: 15–20
MINS

500g (1lb 2oz) white fish, such
as cod or halibut, skin
removed and cut into
bite-sized pieces
Oil spray
3 tbsp finely chopped
coriander (cilantro)
Flaky sea salt

FOR THE MARINADE
2 tbsp rapeseed (canola) oil
(optional)
1 tbsp lemon juice
1½ tbsp garlic and ginger paste
1 tsp ground cumin
1 tsp ground coriander
2 tsp salt
½ tsp ajwain (carom)
seeds (optional)
½ tsp ground turmeric
1 tsp garam masala
1 tbsp Kashmiri chilli powder
(more or less to taste)
1 tbsp dried red chilli flakes
(more or less to taste)
1 tbsp rice flour or cornflour
(cornstarch)
2 tbsp gram flour
1 tsp kasoori methi (dried
fenugreek leaves)

TO SERVE
Chutneys of your choice
Lemon or lime wedges

Add all the marinade ingredients, up to and including the gram flour, to a mixing bowl. Then add the kasoori methi by rubbing it between your fingers for a more intense flavour. Whisk until smooth with no flour lumps. If not adding oil, you might need to add a tablespoon or two of water. The marinade should look wet and thick so that it can coat the fish.

Add the fish and rub the marinade right into the flesh and allow to marinate for 30 minutes–2 hours. If in a hurry, you could go straight to air frying.

When ready to cook, preheat the air fryer to 200°C (400°F). Spray the basket with oil so that the fish doesn't stick and then add the marinated fish and air fry for 15 minutes, turning once halfway through cooking. After 15 minutes, your fish should be cooked through and crispy on the exterior. If not, continue air frying for another few minutes until it is. The fish should be white inside and not opaque or looking raw.

Transfer to a serving plate and serve garnished with the chopped coriander (cilantro) and sprinkled lightly with flaky sea salt. Serve with one or two chutneys or raitas and lemon or lime wedges.

# BEEF CHAPLI KEBABS

SERVES 2–4

**Chapli kebabs are famous deep-fried kebabs from Pakistan. In this recipe, you get all the flavour but without all that oil. I like to divide the meat into two servings, as chapli kebabs are also usually quite large, but you could divide them into smaller patties if you like. With this recipe, you will get a texture closer to a grilled burger than a deep-fried burger, but I actually prefer that. Hopefully you do too.**

PREP TIME: 15 MINS
COOKING TIME: 15 MINS

1 medium onion, very finely
    chopped
1 tomato, finely chopped
2 tbsp finely chopped
    coriander (cilantro)
2 tbsp garlic and ginger paste
3 green bird's eye chillies,
    very finely chopped
1 tbsp dried chilli flakes
1 tsp Kashmiri chilli powder
1 tbsp cumin seeds,
    lightly crushed
1 tbsp coriander seeds,
    lightly crushed
1 tsp garam masala
1 tsp ground black pepper
½ tsp salt, plus extra to taste
1 tbsp roasted gram flour
500g (1lb 2oz) minced (ground)
    beef (preferably 20% fat)
150g (5oz) beef marrow
    (available from most
    butchers and many
    supermarkets), coarsely
    chopped

TO FINISH
1 tomato, thinly sliced
Oil spray
2 limes, quartered
Flaky salt, to taste
Coriander, mint and mango
    chutney (see page 121) or
    sauces of your choice,
    to serve

Place all the chapli kebab ingredients up to and including the minced (ground) beef in a mixing bowl and mix well to combine. You want to break the meat down, so knead it for about 5 minutes until super fine and well combined. The idea here is not only to combine the ingredients but to super-mince the meat. Now add the bone marrow and mix well. Divide the meat mixture into 2–4 patties. Top each patty with one or two slices of tomato and press them in.

When ready to cook, preheat the air fryer to 200°C (400°F). Spray the basket with oil and place the kebabs inside. Spray the tops with oil and cook for 15 minutes. There is no need to turn the kebabs during cooking. Chapli kebabs are usually quite crispy when cooked but if you prefer you could take them out earlier if you like your meat a bit pink.

Season with flaky salt to taste and serve, just as you cooked them, with the tomato slices facing upwards. Serve alongside the lime, which can be squeezed over the kebabs to taste, and coriander, mint and mango chutney or your choice of sauce.

# PANEER PAPAD ROLLS

SERVES 2—4

**The marinade for the paneer in this recipe also happens to be a delicious chutney. I like to serve it as a side for a tandoori lamb and/or chicken. You only need to use enough of the marinade to coat the paneer and then you can use the rest as a dipping sauce for the paneer or other dishes. It offers a delicious blend of hot, savoury, sour and sweet flavours which go so well with so many recipes.**

PREP TIME: 10 MINS,
   PLUS MARINATING
   (OPTIONAL)
COOKING TIME: 10 MINS

125g (4½oz) paneer, cut into
   4 equal strips
4 papads
Oil spray
Rapeseed (canola) oil, for
   brushing (optional)

FOR THE MARINADE AND
   DIPPING SAUCE

1 large bunch of mint,
   leaves picked
1 small bunch of coriander
   (cilantro), leaves picked
200ml (scant 1 cup) smooth
   mango chutney
1–4 green chillies, finely
   chopped
1 garlic clove, finely chopped
Juice of 1 lime
Salt, to taste

Start by preparing the marinade/dipping sauce. Place all the ingredients up to and including the lime juice in a blender and blend to a smooth sauce. You can add a drop of water if needed to assist blending. Season with salt to taste and set aside.

Put the paneer sticks in a bowl and add 2 generous tablespoons of the marinade. You can marinate the paneer for a few hours or go straight to cooking. Reserve the rest of the marinade to use as a dip. The dip is delicious with any air fried meat or slathered over a naan, so if you have any left over, don't throw it away!

Now pour a little water on a plate and soak one of the papads in it for 30 seconds. Transfer to a clean work surface and pat it dry with a paper towel. Place one of the marinated paneer sticks on top and then begin rolling into a cigar shape. You could leave the ends open or fold them in before rolling.

When ready to cook, spray or brush the air fryer basket with oil and place the paneer rolls inside. Spray the tops of the rolls with oil and then air fry at 200°C (400°F) for 7 minutes, turning once halfway through cooking, spraying again with oil. Continue cooking until you are happy with the colour and crispiness. The papad rolls will become crispier as they sit on your serving plate.

Serve with the dipping sauce. As you can see, these paneer papad rolls are really easy to make, so you might want to make seconds while you devour the first batch.

# HARIYALI PANEER AND VEGETABLE SKEWERS

SERVES 2–4

**These paneer skewers make an easy and delicious starter but that's not all! You could add them to a curry sauce; they would be good in any of the curries in this book. I like to add them to butter paneer, which is why I use quite a lot of yoghurt in the marinade. The leftover marinade can be added for extra flavour. If you are just making this as a starter, you could get away with using just 2 tablespoons of yoghurt in the marinade. You will need to soak about five wooden skewers in water for 30 minutes before starting this recipe.**

PREP TIME: 10 MINS,
   PLUS MARINATING
   (OPTIONAL)
COOKING TIME: 10–15
   MINS

250g (9oz) paneer, cut into
   cubes
½ large red (bell) pepper, cut
   into the same sized pieces
   as the paneer
1 medium red onion, cut into
   the same sized pieces as
   the paneer
Oil spray
Raita or hot sauce of your
   choice, to serve

FOR THE MARINADE
30g (1oz) coriander (cilantro)
20g (¾oz) mint leaves
10 fresh or frozen curry leaves
6 green bird's eye chillies,
   roughly chopped (more or
   less to taste)
½ red onion, roughly chopped
1 tbsp ground cumin
1 tsp ground coriander
1 tsp amchoor (dried mango
   powder)
3 tbsp Greek yoghurt

Place all the marinade ingredients, except for the yoghurt, in a blender and blend with just enough water to make a thick paste. The paste needs to be thick, so be careful when adding the water. You only want to add enough water to assist blending, not make it runny. Pour it into a bowl, whisk in the yoghurt and set aside.

Prick each piece of paneer a couple of times with a fork and then place the vegetables and paneer in the marinade and allow to marinate for about 2 hours for best results, or just go straight to cooking.

When ready to cook, preheat the air fryer to 200°C (400°F). Skewer the paneer and vegetables. Spray the cooking basket with oil, place the skewers inside and spray the skewered paneer too.

Air fry for 10 minutes, turning halfway through cooking. When you turn the skewers, be sure to spray the top with more oil spray. The skewers are ready when the exterior is nicely browned or charred to your liking and the centre of the paneer is soft and hot. You can cook the skewers longer if you prefer more of a char. Just keep an eye on them.

You can serve these on a hot plate or wrap a naan around the skewer and pull the hot paneer and vegetables off into the naan. Top with your favourite raita or hot sauce.

# NARGISI KOFTAS

SERVES 2–4

I'm not going to lie and say that this recipe is easy. Most of it is, but when you soft boil eggs in an air fryer, they become difficult (but not impossible) to peel. This isn't a big problem, though – the eggs will be encapsulated into the meat mixture so only you will know if you make a mess of it all. I just wanted to warn you. For this recipe I recommend air frying the eggs for just 10 minutes so they resemble soft boiled eggs. You will be cooking them further in the meat mixture and you don't want those egg yolks really hard. Cooking the eggs for 10 minutes will achieve a jammy texture, as pictured, if you do want a harder yolk, air fry the eggs a couple minutes longer.

PREP TIME: 15 MINS
COOKING TIME: 30 MINS

600g (1lb 5oz) minced (ground) lamb or beef (80:20 meat to fat ratio)
½ red onion, very finely chopped
1 tbsp Garlic, ginger and chilli paste (see page 120)
2 tbsp finely chopped coriander (cilantro)
½ tsp salt
2 tsp Kashmiri chilli powder (more or less to taste)
1 tsp ground coriander
½ tsp ground cumin
½ tsp ground black pepper
½ tsp salt, plus extra to taste
1 egg, beaten

TO FINISH
4 eggs
30g (½ cup) panko breadcrumbs
Oil spray
Chilli raita (see page 101), coriander chutney (see page 99) or other sauce of your choice, to serve

Preheat the air fryer to 130°C/265°F. Place the four eggs directly in the basket and cook for 10 minutes. The eggs will be hot, so use a spoon to transfer them to a bowl of ice-cold water to stop them cooking for 10 minutes. Then carefully peel the egg shells under cold running water and set aside.

While the eggs are resting in the cold water, place all the ingredients for the koftas up to and including the beaten egg in a mixing bowl. Knead the mixture with your hands to break the meat down until it is smooth and fine. This will take a couple of minutes. Both the eggs and meat mixture can be placed in the fridge to cook later if more convenient.

When ready to cook, preheat the air fryer to 200°C (400°F). Divide the meat mixture into four equal balls. Wrap the meat around the whole eggs so that the eggs are right in the centre of the meat. Pour the panko breadcrumbs onto a plate. Spray each of the koftas with oil and then roll them in the breadcrumbs to coat all over. Spray the exterior of each kofta again with oil.

Spray the basket with oil and carefully place the koftas inside. Air fry for 15 minutes, turning once or twice to get an evenly crispy exterior.

Serve with a good chilli raita, green chutney or any sauce of your choice.

# CURRIES

In this section you will find all the most popular
curry house-style curries. The proteins used in each
recipe really are mix and match with the sauces.
If a lamb Madras doesn't appeal to you but a
chicken or paneer version does, then go ahead and
use one of those ingredients instead. The sauces
are all prepared separately to the different proteins,
so you can air fry some chicken tikka, beef, lamb
or paneer and add it to the sauce of your choice
once cooked through and tender. The curries
can all be served with one or more delicious
side dishes which you will find in the
Basics and Side Dishes chapter
starting on page 108.

## COOKING TEMPERATURE

These curries are all cooked at 200°C (400°F) so that they work for all air fryers. Feel free, however, to adjust and use the cooking modes available to you. Just check the curries often and note down how or if you needed to adjust the cooking time using the other cooking modes.

## HOW TO COOK LIGHTER

These recipes were all developed with flavour and appearance in mind. They are not low-calorie, air fry alternatives! I wanted them to look and taste like those you find at Indian restaurants. I do, however, give suggestions on how you can cook these recipes lighter, should you wish to do so. Some of the curries require tempering whole spices in oil. I suggest doing just that but you can always spoon out some of the oil once it has done its job of releasing the flavours from the spices. Don't remove all of the oil, though, as that is the whole point of tempering the spices in the first place. Flavour!

**Cook these curries the way you want!**
Although the recipes were developed just for air fryers, you aren't limited to the simple air fryer. Let's say you have a multi-cooker that has both sauté and air fryer functions. If you would rather, you could sauté the base ingredients, such as onions, (bell) pepper and garlic and ginger paste, in a little oil to soften instead of air frying them. For that matter, you could also sauté your meat, seafood and/or paneer if that is your preferred way of cooking. Go ahead and use a pan on the hob (stove) if you like. Use these air fryer recipes as they are or in the way that's most convenient for you.

## ABOUT THE INGREDIENTS

You might notice that each of these curry recipes calls for a lot of ingredients. You do want your curry to taste amazing after all, don't you? Don't let the amount of ingredients scare you. Most of the elements are repeated in every curry, with different ingredients added to make them into the curries they are. I recommend looking at the ingredients list first and jotting them down so that you can pick them up when you next go shopping.

## MAKING THINGS EASY ON YOURSELF

**Step 1** – At first glance, the recipes might look long and complex. They really aren't. Each of these curries starts in the same way, by preparing a base for the curry. Make one curry and you will see that all of the others start in the same way. The key ingredients for the base are onion, (bell) pepper, garlic and ginger paste, and sometimes chillies. Make just one curry and you'll get the idea.

**Step 2** – Blend the base with the different sauce ingredients. All you need to do is blitz them together and then cook the sauce as explained in the recipe. Some curries call for tempering spices in oil before adding the sauce but they really are very similar at this step.

**Step 3** – Add your protein of choice. You are not limited to the protein listed in the recipe. A lamb curry could very easily be made into a chicken curry by simply substituting the meat. For speed and flavour, I recommend adding pre-air fried tandoori chicken, lamb, beef and or paneer and vegetables, but you could just use a cooked protein like chicken or lamb that you have on hand too. You won't need to alter the recipe as you are just heating the meat through.

# AIR FRYER BASE SAUCE

MAKES 3 PORTIONS, TO SERVE 1–2 EACH

**This recipe is a time saver. You don't need to make this base curry sauce to make any of the curries in this book as they are all made from scratch. It's just a convenient alternative to air frying the sliced onions, (bell) pepper and garlic and ginger paste that are used in most of the curries. Once made, simply divide it into three equal portions which will be roughly 320ml (1¹⁄₃ cups) each. When a recipe says to place all the sauce ingredients in a blender, add one portion of this sauce and all of the other sauce ingredients and omit the air fried 2 onions, half (bell) pepper and the garlic and ginger paste called for in the recipe. Then blend and proceed with the recipe. It freezes well.**

PREP TIME: 5 MINS
COOKING TIME: 30–35
  MINUTES

6 whole brown onions (approx.
  750g/1lb 10oz total)
1½ red (bell) peppers,
  thinly sliced
3 tbsp garlic and ginger paste
½ carrot
500ml (2 cups) chicken, beef or
  vegetable stock

Preheat the air fryer to 200°C (400°F). Place the onions directly in the basket and air fry for 20 minutes. After 20 minutes, add the (bell) peppers and air fry for a further 8 minutes. Then carefully apply the garlic and ginger paste on a couple of the onions and air fry for another 2 minutes.

Remove the onions with tongs and scrape off any garlic and ginger paste into a bowl. The onions should be really soft. Cut off the tip at one end and squeeze out the cooked onion into the bowl. Add the cooked (bell) pepper and whole, uncooked carrot and then blend it all with a stick blender with the stock until smooth. Use as needed. This sauce will keep, covered tightly in the fridge, for 3–4 days. It can be frozen in an airtight container or freezer bag in convenient-sized portions for up to 6 months.

# CHICKEN TIKKA MASALA
SERVES 1–2

**You will be amazed at how good this chicken tikka masala is, and it's really easy to prepare, too. Normally, chicken tikka masala and other restaurant curries are made with a curry house-style base sauce. In this recipe, the air fried onions, pepper, passata and spices do a great job as a base, so the traditional base sauce simply is not needed. All of the following curry recipes use the same or similar base ingredients, so you should get the hang of it quickly if you cook a few.**

PREP TIME: 10 MINS
COOKING TIME: 30 MINS

300g (10½oz) skinless chicken
thighs or breasts, cut into
bite-sized pieces, or Chicken
tikka (see page 90)
Oil spray

FOR THE SAUCE
1–2 tbsp rapeseed (canola) oil
or ghee or oil spray
2 medium onions, thinly sliced
½ red (bell) pepper, thinly sliced
½ tsp salt
1 tbsp garlic and ginger paste
1 tsp sugar
1 tbsp ground almonds
1 tbsp coconut milk powder or
3 tbsp thick coconut milk
125ml (½ cup) unseasoned
passata
1 tbsp curry powder or Mixed
powder (see page 118)
1 tbsp tandoori masala
1 tsp paprika
375ml (1½ cups) warm
chicken stock

FOR THE CURRY
1 tbsp rapeseed (canola) oil
(optional)
1 tbsp butter
70ml (¼ cup) single (light)
cream, plus extra to garnish
½ tsp red food colouring powder
(optional)
1 tsp kasoori methi (dried
fenugreek leaves)
Juice of ½ lemon
½ tsp garam masala
Salt, to taste
3 tbsp finely chopped coriander
(cilantro), to serve

For this recipe, I recommend using the chicken tikka recipe on page 90 for the chicken. You can, however season raw chicken with a little salt to taste and then cook it. Preheat the air fryer to 200°C (400°F) and spray the basket with oil. Add the chicken to the basket and air fry for 10 minutes. Transfer to a plate and set aside.

To make the sauce, mix the oil, onions, (bell) pepper and salt in a mixing bowl, ensuring that the onions are evenly coated. If you are on a reduced-calorie diet, squirt the veggies all over with oil spray instead of adding the oil. Pour it all into the air fryer basket and cook for 10 minutes, shaking the basket halfway through cooking. Carefully add the garlic and ginger paste into the onion mixture for the last 2 minutes of cooking. The onions should look soft and cooked through and you might also see a couple of more crispy bits.

Pour back into the mixing bowl or a blender and add the sugar, ground almonds, coconut, passata, curry powder or mixed powder, tandoori masala, paprika and stock. Blend with a stick blender or in the blender until smooth. Set aside.

Set your air fryer to 200°C (400°F) and place a small cake tin or another suitable metal pan inside your air fryer. Add the 1 tablespoon of oil, if using. The oil will help the curry cook faster but it is optional. If using oil, let it heat for a couple of minutes. Pour in the sauce and cook for 10 minutes.

After 10 minutes, you will notice that some of the sauce is beginning to caramelize on top and around the sides of the pan. Stir this in for more flavour. Add the cooked chicken, butter and cream and cook for another 5 minutes or until the curry is hot enough to serve. Again scrape any caramelized sauce back in.

To finish, add the food colouring if you prefer a red glow. I didn't add any to mine in the photograph opposite. Then add the kasoori methi by rubbing them between your fingers over the sauce. Stir in the lemon juice, garam masala and salt to taste. Taste and adjust the flavours if you like. You might prefer a sweeter flavour, so add more sugar, for example. Garnish with the chopped coriander (cilantro) to serve. If you like, you could also swirl a little more cream over the top.

# CHICKEN KORMA
SERVES 1–2

**Chicken korma is the creamy, sweet curry that people either love or hate. It's great for kids and those who don't like hot curries because there are no spicy ingredients in it. I'm not a big fan of the curry as it's normally served, so I add a few chopped chillies to spice it up and only stir in a pinch of sugar. Every curry in this book can and should be adjusted to taste, and that's how I take a curry house-style korma and turn it into something I enjoy. This, however, is just like those kormas you find at most curry houses.**

PREP TIME: 10 MINS
COOKING TIME: 30 MINS

300g (10½oz) skinless chicken breasts or thighs, cut into bite-sized pieces and cooked
Oil spray
2 medium onions (about 250g/9oz), thinly sliced
½ red (bell) pepper, thinly sliced
1 tbsp rapeseed (canola) oil or oil spray
2 tsp garlic and ginger paste
1 tbsp unseasoned passata
7 cashews, soaked in hot water for 20 minutes
1 tbsp coconut milk powder (optional)
250ml (1 cup) warm chicken stock
1 tbsp ghee
2.5cm (1in) cinnamon stick
2 green cardamom pods, lightly crushed
200ml (¾ cup) thick coconut milk
70ml (¼ cup) single (light) cream
½ tsp garam masala
1–2 tsp sugar, or to taste
¼ tsp rose water (optional)
Salt, to taste

For kormas, I prefer to add simple cooked chicken that has been seasoned with a little salt to taste. If not using pre-cooked chicken, preheat the air fryer to 200°C (400°F) and spray the basket with oil. Place the chicken pieces inside and air fry for 10 minutes until cooked through. Set aside.

To make the sauce, place the onions, (bell) pepper and some salt in a mixing bowl. Top this with the oil and mix it well to coat the veggies with the oil. If you are on a reduced-calorie diet, squirt the veggies all over with oil spray instead of adding the oil. Pour it all directly into the air fryer basket and air fry for 10 minutes, shaking the basket halfway through cooking. Carefully spread the garlic and ginger paste over the veggies for the last 2 minutes of cooking.

Pour it all back into the mixing bowl or a blender and add the passata, the cashews, coconut milk powder, if using, and the chicken stock. Blend with a stick blender or in the blender until smooth. Set aside.

Set your air fryer to 200°C (400°F). Add the ghee to a small cake tin or another suitable metal pan that fits inside your air fryer and let it melt for 2 minutes. The ghee will give the curry a buttery flavour and help it cook faster. Add the cinnamon stick and cardamom pods and close the air fryer to let their flavour infuse into the hot ghee for 2 minutes. Pour in your prepared korma sauce and cook for 10 minutes. After 10 minutes, you will notice that the sauce has darkened a little on top and has caramelized around the sides of the pan. Stir this in for additional flavour.

Pour in the coconut milk and the chicken and cook for a further 5 minutes or until hot enough to serve. Swirl in the cream and cook for another 2 minutes.

To finish, stir in the garam masala and sugar and salt to taste. Just before serving, drizzle in the rose water, if using. Rose water can quickly overpower the dish, so be careful.

# CHICKEN JALFREZI
SERVES 1–2

Jalfrezi curries take a little longer to cook in a single-compartment air fryer because you want to ensure that the vegetables are cooked to perfection. For this reason, you need to cook them separately. Here you have the option to infuse curry leaves and cumin seeds in hot oil. If this doesn't appeal to you, you can air fry a few curry leaves with the (bell) pepper, onion and tomatoes.

PREP TIME: 10 MINS
COOKING TIME: 40 MINS

3–4 tbsp rapeseed (canola) oil or oil spray
300g (10½oz) skinless chicken thighs or breasts, cut into bite-sized pieces, or Chicken tikka (see page 90)
½ green (bell) pepper, cut into 4cm (1½in) squares
½ red or yellow (bell) pepper, cut into 4cm (1½in) squares
½ red onion, cut into 4cm (1½in) squares
2 small tomatoes, quartered
1 tsp cumin seeds (optional)
15 curry leaves (optional)
1 tsp kasoori methi (dried fenugreek leaves)
½ tsp garam masala
3 tbsp chopped coriander (cilantro)
2 limes or lemons, quartered
Salt, to taste

FOR THE SAUCE
2 medium onions, thinly sliced
½ red (bell) pepper, cut in half and seeded
½ tsp salt
4 green finger chillies, sliced in half lengthwise
1 tbsp garlic and ginger paste
125ml (½ cup) unseasoned passata
2 tsp curry powder or Mixed powder (see page 118)
2 tsp tandoori masala
2 tsp Kashmiri chilli powder
250ml (1 cup) warm chicken stock

If you have cooked chicken tikka, skip this step. If cooking raw chicken or raw marinated chicken, preheat the air fryer to 200°C (400°F). Lightly spray your cooking basket with oil and add the chicken in one layer. Air fry for 10–15 minutes, turning halfway through cooking. Transfer to a plate and set aside.

Place the onions, (bell) pepper and salt for the sauce in a mixing bowl and add the chillies. Top with 1 tablespoon of the rapeseed (canola) oil and mix well. If you are on a reduced-calorie diet, squirt the veggies all over with oil spray instead of adding the oil. Pour it all directly into the air fryer basket and air fry for 10 minutes, shaking the basket halfway through cooking. Carefully spread the garlic and ginger paste over the veggies for the last 2 minutes of cooking.

Pour it all back into the mixing bowl or a blender, reserving two of the air fried chillies. Add the passata, curry powder or mixed powder, tandoori masala, chilli powder and stock. Blend with a stick blender or in the blender until smooth. Set aside.

Next, air fry the (bell) peppers, onion and tomatoes for 10 minutes, shaking the basket a couple of times during cooking. Watch this closely as you don't want to overcook the veggies but fry them until they are just cooked through. Transfer to a plate and set aside.

This next step is optional. Pour 1–2 tablespoons of oil into a small cake tin or another suitable metal pan that fits inside your air fryer. Set the air fryer to 200°C (400°F) and heat the oil for 2 minutes. After 2 minutes, add the cumin seeds and curry leaves and stir them into the oil. Cook for 1–3 minutes, checking after 1 minute. If the cumin seeds and curry leaves are sizzling in the oil and fragrant, stop cooking. If not, continue air frying. You can take a few of the crispy fried curry leaves out to use as a garnish if you like.

Pour over the blended sauce and air fry for 10 minutes. If you infused the oil, your sauce will be hot after 10 minutes. If not, it will still be getting warm. The sauce will have browned a little on top and around the sides. Stir that in for added flavour, then add the chicken and cook for a further 5 minutes or until hot enough to serve.

Add the kasoori methi by crumbling it between your fingers, then add the garam masala, chopped coriander and salt to taste. Add the cooked bell peppers, onions and tomatoes and the reserved chillies, along with lemon or lime juice to taste. Air fry for a further 2 minutes before serving.

# CHICKEN CHASNI

**SERVES 1–2**

Chicken chasni is usually served bright red, which is done with food colouring. The colouring adds no flavour, so I'll let you decide whether you want to add it or not. In the chasni opposite, I did! This is a mild curry that is perfect for kids and those who don't like spicy food. You could add some chilli powder or green chillies if you like. I often do but then that isn't a chasni, it's just a delicious spicy curry.

**PREP TIME: 10 MINS**
**COOKING TIME: 30 MINS**

300g (10½oz) skinless chicken thighs or breasts, cut into bite-sized pieces, or Chicken tikka (see page 90)
Oil spray (optional)

**FOR THE CHASNI SAUCE**
2 medium onions (approx. 250g/9oz), thinly sliced
½ red onion, finely chopped
½ red (bell) pepper, thinly sliced
1 tbsp rapeseed (canola) oil or ghee or oil spray
½ tsp salt
1 tbsp garlic and ginger paste
125ml (½ cup) unseasoned passata or tinned (canned) chopped tomatoes
1 tsp ground cumin
1 tsp sweet paprika
1½ tbsp mango chutney
1 tbsp mint sauce (I use Colman's)
1½ tbsp ketchup
250ml (1 cup) warm chicken stock

**TO FINISH**
1 tbsp rapeseed (canola) oil or ghee (optional)
80ml (¼ cup) single (light) cream
Juice of 1 lemon or lime
¼ tsp garam masala
½ tsp red food colouring powder (optional, but needed for a traditional chasni)
2 tbsp finely chopped coriander (cilantro), to garnish
Salt, to taste

If you have cooked chicken tikka, you can skip this step. If cooking raw chicken or raw marinated chicken, preheat the air fryer to 200°C (400°F). Lightly spray your cooking basket with oil and add the chicken in one layer. Air fry for 10–15 minutes, turning halfway through cooking. Transfer to a plate and set aside.

Place the onions, (bell) pepper, oil and salt in a mixing bowl. If you are on a reduced-calorie diet, squirt the veggies all over with oil spray instead of adding the oil. Pour it all into the cooking basket and air fry for 10 minutes, stirring halfway through cooking. Carefully spread the garlic and ginger paste over the veggies for the last 2 minutes of cooking.

Pour it all back into the mixing bowl or a blender and add the remaining sauce ingredients. Blend with a stick blender or in the blender until smooth. Set aside.

Place a small cake tin or another suitable metal pan that fits into your air fryer. For a faster cook and more authentic Indian restaurant curry appearance, heat the 1 tablespoon of oil in the pan for 2 minutes. Pour the blended sauce into the pan and air fry for 10 minutes.

If you used hot oil, your sauce will be quite hot after 10 minutes but warm if not. The top and sides of the sauce will have darkened some. That is flavour so stir it in. Stir in the chicken and continue cooking for another 5 minutes, by which time the sauce should be almost hot enough to serve. Keep cooking until it is hot.

Once the sauce is good and hot, stir in the cream, lemon or lime juice, garam masala and food colouring, if using, and cook for another 2 minutes or until hot enough to serve. Season with salt to taste and garnish with the chopped coriander (cilantro).

# CHICKEN REZALA

SERVES 1–2

**Rezala is another of the curry house curries that goes really well with air fried tandoori chicken. Having this on hand will save you about 10 minutes of cooking time, so it is a good recipe to keep on standby. Rezala curries are similar to chicken tikka masala but they are easier to prepare, not as sweet and a little spicier. All of these things can be adjusted to taste if you like.**

PREP TIME: 10 MINS
COOKING TIME: 30 MINS

300g (10½oz) skinless chicken thighs or breasts, cut into bite-sized pieces, or Chicken tikka (see page 90)
Oil spray (optional)

FOR THE SAUCE
2 medium onions (approx. 250g/9oz), thinly sliced
½ red (bell) pepper, thinly sliced
½ tsp salt
1 tbsp rapeseed (canola) oil or ghee or oil spray
1 tbsp garlic and ginger paste
125ml (½ cup) unseasoned passata or tinned (canned) chopped tomatoes
1 tbsp curry powder or Mixed powder (see page 118)
1 tsp Kashmiri chilli powder (more or less to taste)
250ml (1 cup) warm chicken stock

TO FINISH
2 tbsp rapeseed (canola) oil or ghee or oil spray
½ red onion, finely chopped
2–3 green finger chillies, finely chopped
70ml (¼ cup) single (light) cream
¼ tsp garam masala
2 tbsp finely chopped coriander (cilantro), plus extra leaves to garnish
1 tbsp cold butter, plus extra (optional) to serve
Salt, to taste

If you have cooked chicken tikka, you can skip this step. If cooking raw chicken or raw marinated chicken, preheat the air fryer to 200°C (400°F). Lightly spray your cooking basket with oil and add the chicken in one layer. Air fry for 10–15 minutes, turning halfway through cooking. Transfer to a plate and set aside.

Place the onions, (bell) pepper and salt in a bowl with the oil. If you are on a reduced-calorie diet, squirt the veggies all over with oil spray instead of adding the oil. Mix well with your hands and then pour it all into the cooking basket. Air fry for 10 minutes, stirring halfway through cooking. Spread the garlic and ginger paste over the veggies for the last 2 minutes of cooking.

Pour it all back into the mixing bowl or a blender and add the passata, curry powder, Kashmiri chilli powder and stock. Blend with a stick blender or in the blender until smooth. Set aside.

Pour the 2 tablespoons of oil into a small cake tin or another suitable metal pan that fits inside your air fryer. If you are on a reduced-calorie diet, simply spray the chopped onion and chillies to coat instead. If using oil, it should take about 2 minutes to heat up. Add the red onion and fry for 3 minutes. Then stir in the chillies and continue frying for a further 2 minutes to soften.

Pour the blended sauce into the pan and stir well to combine. Air fry for 10 minutes. If you used hot oil, your sauce will be quite hot after 10 minutes but getting warm if you didn't. The top will be a darker brown and that is flavour, so stir it in.

Add the cooked chicken and cook for a further 5 minutes or until hot enough to serve. To finish, swirl in the cream, garam masala, coriander (cilantro) and butter and cook for a further 2 minutes or until the sauce is hot and the chicken is heated through. Season with salt to taste and garnish with a little chopped coriander and even a little more butter if you like.

# CHICKEN CHILLI GARLIC
SERVES 1–2

**Whenever I go out for a curry, chicken chilli garlic has to be on my table. If you're a fan of garlicky and spicy curries, this is one you need to make. How garlicky and spicy you make it is down to your personal preference, but this recipe will get you on the right course. Then taste and adjust.**

PREP TIME: 10 MINS
COOKING TIME: 25 MINS

300g (10½oz) skinless chicken thighs or breasts, cut into bite-sized pieces, or Chicken tikka (see page 90)
Oil spray
2 tbsp rapeseed (canola) oil or ghee or oil spray
8 garlic cloves, sliced into thin slivers
2–3 green finger chillies, finely chopped (more or less, to taste)
½ red onion, finely chopped

FOR THE SAUCE
2 medium onions (approx. 250g/9oz), thinly sliced
½ red (bell) pepper, thinly sliced
½ tsp salt
1 tbsp rapeseed (canola) oil or ghee or oil spray
1 tbsp garlic and ginger paste
125ml (½ cup) unseasoned passata or tinned (canned) chopped tomatoes
1 tbsp curry powder or Mixed powder (see page 118)
1 tbsp tandoori masala
1–2 tsp Kashmiri chilli powder (more or less to taste)
1 tbsp tomato purée (paste)
250ml (1 cup) warm chicken stock

TO FINISH
½ tsp kasoori methi (dried fenugreek leaves)
Coriander (cilantro), leaves picked
Dried garlic flakes (optional)
1 lime, quartered
Salt, to taste

If you have cooked chicken tikka, you can skip this step. If cooking raw chicken or raw marinated chicken, preheat the air fryer to 200°C (400°F). Lightly spray your cooking basket with oil and add the chicken in one layer. Air fry for 10–15 minutes, turning halfway through cooking. Transfer to a plate and set aside.

Place the onions, (bell) pepper, salt and oil in a mixing bowl. If you are on a reduced-calorie diet, squirt the veggies all over with oil spray instead of adding the oil. Pour it all into the cooking basket and air fry for 10 minutes, stirring or shaking the basket halfway through cooking. Carefully spread the garlic and ginger paste over it all for the last 2 minutes of cooking.

Pour it all back into the mixing bowl or a blender and add the remaining sauce ingredients. Blend with a stick blender or in the blender until smooth. Set aside.

Pour the 2 tablespoons of oil into a small cake tin or another suitable metal pan that fits inside your air fryer. If you are on a reduced-calorie diet, spray the garlic with oil to coat instead but you will need to keep a close eye on it as it cooks so that it doesn't burn. Pour the slivered garlic into the pan and air fry for about 3 minutes, stirring a couple of times and watching it carefully. You only want to soften and lightly brown the garlic slivers. Once you are happy with the garlic, add the chillies and red onion and air fry for about 3 more minutes, stirring at least once.

Pour your smooth curry sauce over it all and stir well to combine. Then air fry at 200°C (400°F) for 10 minutes. After 10 minutes, you will notice that the sauce is browning, even caramelizing on top and around the sides of the pan. If you used oil, the sauce will be quite hot and nicely warmed if not. Stir well, add your chicken and continue air frying for another 5 minutes to heat it through. If your curry is not hot enough to serve at this stage, just let it air fry for another couple of minutes until it is.

To finish, add the kasoori methi by rubbing it between your fingers and season with salt to taste. Garnish with the chopped coriander (cilantro) and the dried garlic flakes, if using, and add lime juice to taste or just add the lime juice at the table.

# CHICKEN PATHIA
SERVES 1—2

**Pathia curries are sweet and sour in flavour. Although they are usually quite mild, they can be rather spicy at some restaurants, so feel free to add more chilli powder to taste. The curry was originally developed by curry house chefs to compete with the sweet and sour Chinese dishes that were popular at the time.**

PREP TIME: 10 MINS
COOKING TIME: 25 MINS

300g (10½oz) skinless chicken thighs or breasts, cut into bite-sized pieces, or Chicken tikka (see page 90)
Oil spray (optional)

FOR THE SAUCE
2 medium onions (approx. 250g/9oz), thinly sliced
½ red (bell) pepper, thinly sliced
½ tsp salt
1 tbsp rapeseed (canola) oil or ghee or oil spray
1 tbsp garlic and ginger paste
1 tbsp tomato purée (paste)
125ml (½ cup) unseasoned passata or tinned (canned) chopped tomatoes
1 tbsp curry powder or Mixed powder (see page 118)
½ tsp Kashmiri chilli powder (more or less to taste)
250ml (1 cup) warm chicken stock
1 tbsp sugar
2 tsp mango chutney
½ tsp tamarind concentrate or tamarind sauce

TO FINISH
2 tbsp rapeseed (canola) oil or oil spray
½ small red onion, finely chopped
½ tsp kasoori methi (dried fenugreek leaves)
½ tsp garam masala
Juice of 1 lemon (more or less to taste)
2 tbsp finely chopped coriander (cilantro)
Salt, to taste

If you have cooked chicken tikka, you can skip this step. If cooking raw chicken or raw marinated chicken, preheat the air fryer to 200°C (400°F). Lightly spray your cooking basket with oil and add the chicken in one layer. Air fry for 10–15 minutes, turning halfway through cooking. Transfer to a plate and set aside.

Place the onions, (bell) pepper and salt in a bowl and add the oil. If you are on a reduced-calorie diet, squirt the veggies all over with oil spray instead of adding the oil. Mix well with your hands or a spoon. Pour it all into the cooking basket and air fry for 10 minutes, stirring halfway through cooking. Carefully spread the garlic and ginger paste over the veggies for the last minute or two of cooking.

Pour it all back into the mixing bowl or a blender and add the remaining sauce ingredients. Blend with a stick blender or in the blender until smooth. Set aside.

Pour the 2 tablespoons of oil into a small cake tin or another suitable metal pan that fits inside your air fryer. If you are on a reduced-calorie diet, simply spray the chopped red onion with oil to coat instead. Add the red onion and air fry for 3 minutes or until the onion is turning soft. Pour your prepared curry sauce over the onion and air fry for 10 minutes.

If you used the oil, after 10 minutes your sauce should be quite hot, and getting warm if you used oil spray. Add the cooked chicken, stir it in and continue cooking for another 5 minutes or until the curry is hot enough to serve and the chicken is heated through.

To finish, stir in the kasoori methi, garam masala and add salt and lemon juice to taste. Serve garnished with the coriander (cilantro).

# CHICKEN CEYLON

SERVES 1–2

**Chicken Ceylon is a curry house favourite, offering a taste of Sri Lanka. It is the perfect mix of savoury, sweet, sour and spicy flavours.**

PREP TIME: 10 MINS
COOKING TIME: 20 MINS

300g (10½oz) skinless chicken thighs or breasts, cut into bite-sized pieces, or Chicken tikka (see page 90)
Oil spray (optional)
½ tsp kasoori methi (dried fenugreek leaves)
½ tsp garam masala
Juice of 1 lime
2 tbsp finely chopped coriander (cilantro), to garnish
Salt, to taste

FOR THE SAUCE
2 medium onions, thinly sliced
½ red (bell) pepper, thinly sliced
½ tsp salt
1 tbsp rapeseed (canola) oil or ghee, or oil spray
1 tbsp garlic and ginger paste
125ml (½ cup) unseasoned passata
1 tbsp curry powder or Mixed powder (see page 118)
½ tsp black pepper
½ tsp Kashmiri chilli powder
250ml (1 cup) warm chicken stock
150ml (scant ⅔ cup) thick coconut milk
10 cashews, soaked in water for 10 minutes or longer
½ tsp sugar (or to taste)
2 tsp mango chutney
½ tsp tamarind concentrate

FOR THE TEMPERING
2 tbsp rapeseed (canola) oil
15 fresh or frozen curry leaves
2 green finger chillies, finely chopped
1 star anise
2 green cardamom pods, lightly bruised
2.5cm (1in) cinnamon stick
½ small red onion, finely chopped

If you have cooked chicken tikka, you can skip this step. If cooking raw chicken or raw marinated chicken, preheat the air fryer to 200°C (400°F). Lightly spray your cooking basket with oil and add the chicken in one layer. Air fry for 10–15 minutes, turning halfway through cooking. Transfer to a plate and set aside.

Place the onions, (bell) pepper and salt in a bowl and add the oil. If you are on a reduced-calorie diet, squirt the veggies all over with oil spray instead of adding the oil. Mix well with your hands or a spoon. Pour it all into the cooking basket and air fry for 10 minutes, stirring halfway through cooking. Carefully add the garlic and ginger paste for the last 2 minutes of cooking.

Pour it all back into the mixing bowl or a blender and add the remaining sauce ingredients. Blend with a stick blender or in the blender until smooth. Set aside.

Pour the oil for tempering into a small cake tin or another suitable metal pan that fits inside your air fryer. Heat the oil for 1–2 minutes and then stir in all the tempering ingredients. If you are on a reduced-calorie diet, you could generously spray these ingredients with oil instead. If doing this, I recommend not adding the whole spices but instead adding a pinch of ground cinnamon and ground cardamom to the sauce. Air fry for about 3 minutes or until fragrant, opening the drawer to stir a couple of times. Pour in the prepared sauce and heat for 10 minutes.

If you used oil, after 10 minutes the sauce will be quite hot but warm if you used oil spray. The top and sides will have darkened and caramelized a little. Stir that in for additional flavour. Add the chicken and continue air frying for another 5 minutes to heat it through, or until the curry is hot enough to serve.

To finish, add the kasoori methi by rubbing it between your fingers over the sauce and stir in the garam masala. Add salt to taste, then squeeze in the lime juice to taste and serve garnished with the chopped coriander (cilantro).

# CHICKEN PASANDA

SERVES 1–2

Curry house-style pasandas are really rich, sweet and mild. The coconut milk powder used in this recipe gives a delicious flavour of coconut. It's used a lot in restaurant kitchens and can be found online and at Indian grocers. You could leave it out and add more coconut milk to taste. Pasanda curries are usually garnished with flaked (slivered) almonds. For added flavour, you could toast them in your air fryer basket for 4–5 minutes at 200°C (400°F).

PREP TIME: 10 MINS
COOKING TIME: 20 MINS

300g (10½oz) skinless chicken
thighs or breasts, cut into
bite-sized pieces, or Chicken
tikka (see page 90)
Oil spray (optional)

FOR THE SAUCE
2 medium onions (about
250g/9oz), thinly sliced
½ red (bell) pepper, thinly
sliced
½ tsp salt
1 tbsp rapeseed (canola) oil
or ghee or oil spray
1 generous tsp garlic and
ginger paste
2 tsp tomato purée (paste)
or unseasoned passata
70ml (¼ cup) red wine
150ml (scant ⅔ cup)
chicken stock

TO FINISH
2 tbsp rapeseed (canola) oil
1½ tbsp coconut milk powder
(optional)
1½ tbsp ground almonds
1 tbsp sugar
10 raisins
100ml (scant ½ cup) thick
coconut milk
70ml (¼ cup) single (light)
cream (more or less
to taste)
4 tbsp toasted flaked (slivered)
almonds, to garnish
(optional)
Salt, to taste

If you have cooked chicken tikka, you can skip this step. If cooking raw chicken or raw marinated chicken, preheat the air fryer to 200°C (400°F). Lightly spray your cooking basket with oil and add the chicken in one layer. Air fry for 10–15 minutes, turning halfway through cooking. Transfer to a plate and set aside.

Place the onions, (bell) pepper and salt in a bowl and add the oil. If you are on a reduced-calorie diet, squirt the veggies all over with oil spray instead of adding the oil. Pour it all into the basket and air fry for 10 minutes, stirring halfway through cooking. Carefully add the garlic and ginger paste on top of the veggies for the last 2 minutes of cooking.

Pour it all back into the mixing bowl or a blender and add the remaining sauce ingredients. Blend with a stick blender or in the blender until smooth. Set aside.

Pour the 2 tablespoons of oil into a small cake tin or another suitable metal pan that fits inside your air fryer. Heat it for 2 minutes, then stir in the coconut milk powder, if using, ground almonds, sugar and raisins and air fry for another minute, stirring well to combine. Pour in the prepared sauce, stir well and cook for 10 minutes. After 10 minutes, you might notice that the sauce has darkened a little on top and caramelized around the edges. Stir that in for additional flavour.

Add the cooked chicken, stir it in to cook for another 5 minutes or until the curry is hot enough to serve. Stir in the coconut milk and cream, leaving a little cream to drizzle over the finished curry. Season with salt to taste and cook for another 2 minutes. Serve garnished with toasted flaked (slivered) almonds, if you like.

# CHICKEN METHI
SERVES 1–2

**Chicken methi has to be one of my favourite curries. It's just different, and although you can taste the fenugreek in the curry, it is by no means overpowering.**

PREP TIME: 10 MINS
COOKING TIME: 20 MINS

Approx. 60g (2¼oz) methi
    (fenugreek leaves)
300g (10½oz) skinless chicken
    thighs or breasts, cut into
    bite-sized pieces, or Chicken
    tikka (see page 90)
Oil spray (optional)

FOR THE SAUCE
2 medium onions (approx.
    250g/9oz), thinly sliced
½ red (bell) pepper, thinly
    sliced
½ tsp salt
1 tbsp rapeseed (canola) oil
    or ghee or oil spray
1 tbsp garlic and ginger paste
1 tbsp tomato purée (paste)
125ml (½ cup) unseasoned
    passata or tinned (canned)
    chopped tomatoes
1 tbsp curry powder or Mixed
    powder (see page 118)
½ tsp Kashmiri chilli powder
    (more or less to taste)
250ml (1 cup) warm
    chicken stock

TO FINISH
2 tbsp rapeseed (canola) oil
    or ghee
1 star anise
1 Indian bay leaf (cassia leaf)
½ tsp coriander seeds
½ tsp fennel seeds
½ onion, finely chopped
2 tbsp natural yoghurt
½ tsp kasoori methi (dried
    fenugreek leaves), plus extra
    to garnish
½ tsp garam masala
2 tbsp coriander (cilantro),
    finely chopped
Juice of 1 lemon (more or less
    to taste)
Salt, to taste

Finely chop the methi leaves and place in a bowl with ½ teaspoon of salt. Mix well and leave to sit while you prepare the other ingredients. This step will remove the bitter flavour of the leaves.

If you have cooked chicken tikka, you can skip this step. If cooking raw chicken or raw marinated chicken, preheat the air fryer to 200°C (400°F). Lightly spray your cooking basket with oil and add the chicken in one layer. Air fry for 10–15 minutes, turning halfway through cooking. Transfer to a plate and set aside.

Place the onions and (bell) pepper in a bowl and stir in the salt and oil. If you are on a reduced-calorie diet, squirt the veggies all over with oil spray instead of adding the oil. Pour into the cooking basket and air fry for 10 minutes, stirring halfway through. Carefully spread the garlic and ginger paste over it all for the last 2 minutes of cooking.

Pour it all back into the mixing bowl or a blender and add the remaining sauce ingredients. Blend with a stick blender or in the blender until smooth. Set aside.

Now add the 2 tablespoons of oil to a small cake tin or another suitable metal pan that fits inside your air fryer. Heat the oil for 2 minutes, then add the star anise, Indian bay leaf, coriander and fennel seeds and air fry for a minute or two or until fragrant. Add the chopped onion and fry for 3 minutes or until soft.

Pour your prepared curry sauce over it all and air fry for 10 minutes. After 10 minutes, the sauce will be hot. Pick up the salted methi leaves and squeeze out all the excess moisture. Add the leaves and chicken to the sauce and cook for another 5 minutes or until the curry is hot enough to serve.

To finish, whisk in the yoghurt and then add the kasoori methi, garam masala and coriander. Stir well and season with salt to taste. Garnish with the kasoori methi and add lemon juice to taste.

# CHICKEN DHANSAK
SERVES 1–2

**When it comes to fans of curry house-style dhansak, there are two groups: those who like pineapple and those who don't. In this recipe, you make the curry in the same way, regardless of which group you belong to. The pineapple is added at the end of cooking on top of the sauce to char and caramelize a bit. Of course, if you don't like pineapple in your curry, don't do that.**

PREP TIME: 10 MINS
COOKING TIME: 30 MINS

300g (10½oz) skinless chicken thighs or breasts, cut into bite-sized pieces, or Chicken tikka (see page 90)
Oil spray (optional)

FOR THE SAUCE
2 medium onions (approx. 250g/9oz), thinly sliced
1 red (bell) pepper, cut in half and seeded
½ tsp salt
1 tbsp rapeseed (canola) oil or oil spray
1 tbsp garlic and ginger paste
3 green finger chillies, sliced in half lengthwise
125ml (½ cup) unseasoned passata
1 tbsp curry powder or Mixed powder (see page 118)
2 tsp Kashmiri chilli powder
½ tsp ground cumin
½ tsp paprika
250ml (1 cup) warm chicken stock
70ml (¼ cup) pineapple juice
2 tsp tamarind sauce

TO FINISH
2 tbsp rapeseed (canola) oil (optional)
90g (½ cup) Tarka dal (see page 122)
2 tinned (canned) pineapple rings
2 tsp lemon juice
2 tbsp coriander (cilantro), to garnish
Salt, to taste

If you have cooked chicken tikka, you can skip this step. If cooking raw chicken or raw marinated chicken, preheat the air fryer to 200°C (400°F). Lightly spray your cooking basket with oil and add the chicken in one layer. Air fry for 10–15 minutes, turning halfway through cooking. When the chicken is just cooked through and has a nice char on the exterior, tip it all into a bowl and set aside.

Place the onions, (bell) pepper and salt in a mixing bowl and mix well to combine with the oil. If you are on a reduced-calorie diet, squirt the veggies all over with oil spray instead of adding the oil. Pour it all into the air fryer basket and cook for 10 minutes, shaking or stirring well halfway through cooking. Carefully add the garlic and ginger paste on top of the veggies for the last 2 minutes of cooking.

Pour it all back into the mixing bowl or a blender and add the remaining sauce ingredients. Blend with a stick blender or in the blender until smooth. Set aside.

Adding oil at this stage is optional but it will help the curry cook faster and will give it a nice curry house glow. If adding oil, pour the 2 tablespoons of the oil into a small cake tin or another suitable metal pan that fits inside your air fryer. Heat the oil for a couple of minutes, then pour in the blended sauce and cooked lentils and cook for 10 minutes.

If you added oil, after 10 minutes your sauce will be quite hot, and warm if not. The top will have darkened a little and you might see some caramelization around the edges of the pan. Stir all this in for added flavour. Then add the chicken, push it right into the sauce and top with a couple of pineapple rings, if using. Continue cooking for another 5 minutes or until the sauce is hot enough to serve. It will not hurt the sauce to cook longer, so if you want to char your pineapple a little more, do it. Then season with salt and lemon juice to taste. Garnish with the chopped coriander (cilantro) to serve.

# CHICKEN CHAAT

SERVES 1–2

**Chicken chaat is a unique curry house-style curry that calls for lots of chaat masala, which is available at Indian grocers and online. If you haven't tried it before, you might be a bit wary about using it but, believe me, it is good! Chaat masala has an aroma of sulphur because it is made with black salt. Another thing that makes this curry really good is the use of fresh cucumber, chickpeas and tomato, which are stirred in right at the end of cooking. This curry is almost always served with Chicken tikka (see page 90) but you could just air fry some chicken if you're in a rush.**

PREP TIME: 10 MINS
COOKING TIME: 20 MINS

300g (10½oz) skinless chicken thighs or breasts, cut into bite-sized pieces, or Chicken tikka (see page 90)
2–3 tbsp rapeseed (canola) oil (optional) or oil spray

FOR THE SAUCE
2 medium onions (approx. 250g/9oz), thinly sliced
½ red (bell) pepper, thinly sliced
½ tsp salt
1 tbsp rapeseed (canola) oil or oil spray
1 tbsp garlic and ginger paste
125ml (½ cup) unseasoned passata
1 tbsp curry powder or Mixed powder (see page 118)
1 tsp Kashmiri chilli powder
1 tbsp chaat masala
250ml (1 cup) warm chicken stock

TO FINISH
½ red onion, finely chopped
¼ English cucumber, seeded and roughly chopped
1 tomato, quartered
4 tbsp cooked chickpeas (garbanzo beans)
½ tsp garam masala
½ red (bell) pepper, roughly chopped
Salt, to taste

If you have cooked chicken tikka, you can skip this step. If cooking raw chicken or raw marinated chicken, preheat the air fryer to 200°C (400°F). Season the chicken with salt. Lightly spray your cooking basket with oil and add the chicken in one layer. Air fry for 10–15 minutes, turning halfway through cooking. When the chicken is just cooked through and has a nice char on the exterior, pour it all into a bowl and set aside.

Place the onions, (bell) pepper, salt and oil in a mixing bowl and mix well. If you are on a reduced-calorie diet, squirt the veggies all over with oil spray instead of adding the oil. Pour it all into the air fryer basket and cook for 10 minutes, shaking or stirring well halfway through cooking. Carefully add the garlic and ginger paste on top of the veggies for the last 2 minutes of cooking.

Pour it all back into the mixing bowl or a blender and add the passata, curry powder, Kashmiri chilli powder, chaat masala and stock. Blend with a stick blender or in the blender until smooth. Set aside.

Place a small cake tin or another suitable metal pan in your air fryer and add the 2–3 tablespoons of oil. If you are on a reduced-calorie diet, simply spray the chopped red onion and red bell pepper to coat. If using oil, it should take about 2 minutes to heat up. Add the chopped red onion and bell pepper and fry for 3 minutes.

Pour in your prepared sauce and cook for 10 minutes. If you used oil, the sauce will be quite hot after 10 minutes and warm if you used spray. Add the cooked chicken and air fry for another 5 minutes or until the sauce and chicken are hot enough to serve. Stir in the cucumber, tomato, chickpeas (garbanzo beans) and garam masala and stir well to combine. Cook for another 2 minutes and then season with salt to taste. Serve.

# CHICKEN BIRYANI
SERVES 2

For this recipe, you need to use 2 cups of par-cooked Basmati rice. The easiest way to do this is to rinse the rice in several changes of water to remove the excess starch. Soak it for 30 minutes and then boil it in lightly salted water for about 7 minutes or until about 80 per cent cooked. You could also use the air fryer rice recipe on page 110 and remove the rice when it is about 80 per cent cooked. There will be some water remaining in the pan, which you will need to strain. Either way you cook your rice, the result is a proper dum biryani but cooked in a fraction of the time.

PREP TIME: 15 MINS,
    PLUS MARINATING
    (OPTIONAL)
COOKING TIME: 30 MINS

300g (10½oz) skinless chicken thighs or breasts, cut into bite-sized pieces
1 tbsp garlic and ginger paste
3 green finger chillies, finely chopped
½ tsp salt
2 tsp Kashmiri chilli powder
½ tsp ground turmeric
1 tsp garam masala
Juice of 1 lemon
210ml (1 cup) natural yoghurt, whisked
200g (7oz) tinned (canned) chopped tomatoes
2 tbsp melted ghee
A pinch of saffron
Oil spray (optional)
450g (2 cups) hot par-cooked rice (see intro)
100g (1 generous cup) fried onions (shop-bought is fine or see page 120)
5 tbsp finely chopped coriander (cilantro)
20 mint leaves, finely chopped, plus extra leaves to serve
Cucumber raita (see page 93), to serve (optional)

Place the chicken pieces in a mixing bowl and add the garlic and ginger paste, green chillies, salt, chilli powder, turmeric, garam masala and lemon juice. Mix well to coat and set aside for 20 minutes or go straight to the next step.

Cover the marinated chicken with the yoghurt and tomatoes and again stir well to combine. Allow to marinate in the fridge for 30 minutes or overnight. The longer, the better, but if time is an issue you could go straight to cooking.

Transfer the chicken from the marinade to another bowl, shaking off any excess marinade. Retain the marinade! In a small cup, mix the melted ghee with the saffron and set aside to infuse.

Pour half of the par-cooked rice into a small cake tin or another suitable metal pan that fits inside your air fryer. If using a pan that is not non-stick, spray it lightly with oil first. Cover the rice in the pan with a handful of fried onions, half of the remaining marinade and half of the chopped coriander (cilantro) and mint. Top this with the remaining rice and then cover it with the remaining marinade, fried onions, coriander and mint.

Place the chicken pieces on top, pressing them into the top layer of rice and then drizzle it all with the saffron-infused ghee. Cover the pan tightly (if you don't have a lid for your pan, wrap it all up with foil) and place it in your air fryer to cook at 200°C (400°F) for 5 minutes. After 5 minutes, reduce the temperature to 150°C (300°F) to continue cooking for another 12 minutes. After 12 minutes, remove the lid (or foil). The chicken will probably be a bit raw on top. That's good!

Increase the heat to 200°C (400°F). Move the chicken around a bit and air fry for another 8–10 minutes. This will give the chicken a light char and cook it through. Lightly move the rice and chicken around in the pan to separate the rice grains. Do not do this too harshly or the rice will split, so be delicate!

Scatter with the mint, serve immediately and enjoy. I like to serve this biryani with a cucumber raita.

# LAMB DOPIAZA

SERVES 1–2

**Dopiaza translates to 'two onions', so dopiaza curries are cooked with onions in two ways. I think you could probably say that about many curries, but with this dish, the onion is one of the dominant flavours in the sauce, because lightly charred onion petals are added just before serving. You need to pre-cook the lamb using either my Lamb tikka recipe (see page 93) or simply season some lamb as you wish and cook it.**

PREP TIME: 10 MINS
COOKING TIME: 30 MINS

300g (10½oz) Lamb tikka (see page 93) or cooked lamb, cut into bite-sized pieces
Oil spray
1 small onion, quartered and then broken into petals
1 tbsp rapeseed (canola) oil (optional)
2 tbsp natural yoghurt
½ tsp garam masala
½ tsp kasoori methi (dried fenugreek leaves)
2 tbsp finely chopped coriander (cilantro)
Salt, to taste

FOR THE SAUCE
2 medium onions, thinly sliced
1 red (bell) pepper, cut in half and seeded
½ tsp salt
1 tbsp rapeseed (canola) oil or oil spray
1 tbsp garlic and ginger paste
3 green finger chillies, finely chopped
1 tbsp curry powder or Mixed powder (see page 118)
1 tsp Kashmiri chilli powder
1 tsp ground cumin
½ tsp ground coriander
½ tsp paprika
125ml (½ cup) unseasoned passata
250ml (1 cup) warm meat stock

FOR THE TEMPERING
2 tbsp rapeseed (canola) oil
1 tsp cumin seeds
½ tsp coriander seeds, roughly chopped
2 green cardamom pods, bruised

If you haven't already cooked the lamb tikka, do so now. Preheat the air fryer to 200°C (400°F). Spray the basket with oil and place the marinated or seasoned lamb inside to cook for about 15 minutes, turning once. When it's tender, transfer it to a plate. Set aside.

Place the onion petals in a mixing bowl and add the rapeseed (canola) oil. Rub the oil into the onion petals. If you are on a reduced-calorie diet, squirt the veggies all over with oil spray instead of adding the oil. Spray the basket with oil and then place the onion petals in it. Air fry for 5–8 minutes or until the sides of the onion petals are beginning to char and the onion is soft. Transfer to a plate and set aside.

Place the sliced onions, (bell) pepper and salt for the sauce in a mixing bowl and mix well to combine with the oil. If you are on a reduced-calorie diet, you can spray these veggies liberally with oil to coat. Pour it all into the air fryer basket and cook for 10 minutes, stirring halfway through cooking. Carefully add the garlic and ginger paste on top of the veggies for the last 2 minutes of cooking.

Pour it all back into the mixing bowl or a blender and add the remaining sauce ingredients. Blend with a stick blender or in the blender until smooth. Set aside.

Now pour the oil for tempering into a small cake tin or another suitable metal pan that fits inside your air fryer. Heat it for 2 minutes and then stir in the cumin and coriander seeds and cardamom pods. Fry for another minute or two until the oil and spices are bubbling away nicely and you can smell their aroma.

Pour the blended sauce over the spices, along with the cooked lamb and any juices that accumulated, stirring well so that the lamb is right down in the sauce. Air fry for 10 minutes. After 10 minutes, the sauce will be hot but probably not hot enough to serve yet. The top of the sauce will have darkened a little and you might see some caramelization around the edges of the pan. Stir it all in for additional flavour.

To finish, stir in the yoghurt, garam masala, kasoori methi, coriander (cilantro) and salt to taste. Then return the fried onion petals to the top of the curry and air fry for another 2–5 minutes or until the curry is hot enough to serve. Stir well then serve straight away.

# LAMB ROGAN JOSH
SERVES 1–2

**Rogan josh has to be one of the most popular curry house curries that uses red meat. This recipe has little in common with more traditional rogan josh curries in India and Pakistan but if you like this curry from your local Indian curry house, you will recognize the flavour immediately. Although normally served with lamb, this sauce is really good with other proteins such as Chicken tikka (see page 90) or paneer.**

PREP TIME: 10 MINS
COOKING TIME: 30 MINS

300g (10½oz) Lamb tikka
  (see page 93)
Oil spray (optional)

FOR THE SAUCE
2 medium onions (about
  250g/9oz), thinly sliced
1 red (bell) pepper, cut in half
  and seeded
1 tbsp rapeseed (canola) oil or
  oil spray
½ tsp salt
1 tbsp garlic and ginger paste
1 tbsp curry powder or
  Mixed powder (see page 118)
½ tsp Kashmiri chilli powder
½ tsp ground cumin
½ tsp ground coriander
1½ tbsp paprika
5 cashews
150ml (scant ⅔ cup)
  unseasoned passata
250ml (1 cup) warm meat stock

TO FINISH
2 tbsp rapeseed (canola) oil
  (optional)
2 tbsp natural yoghurt
½ tsp kasoori methi (dried
  fenugreek leaves)
½ tsp garam masala
1 tomato, quartered
2 tbsp finely chopped
  coriander (cilantro)
½ small red onion, finely diced
Salt, to taste
Chilli raita (optional; see page
  101)

If you haven't already cooked the lamb tikka, do so now. Preheat the air fryer to 200°C (400°F). Spray the basket with oil and place the marinated or seasoned lamb inside to cook for about 15 minutes, turning once. When it's tender, transfer it to a plate. Set aside.

Place the onions, (bell) pepper, oil and salt in a mixing bowl. If you are on a reduced-calorie diet, squirt the veggies all over with oil spray instead of adding the oil. Mix well. Pour it into the cooking basket and fry for 10 minutes, stirring halfway through cooking. Carefully spread the garlic and ginger paste over the veggies for the last 2 minutes of cooking.

Pour it all back into the mixing bowl or a blender and add the remaining sauce ingredients. Blend with a stick blender or in the blender until smooth. Set aside.

Pour the 2 tablespoons of oil into a small cake tin or another suitable metal pan that fits inside your air fryer. Heat at 200°C (400°F) for 2 minutes. If you are on a reduced-calorie diet, you don't have to add the oil to the pan but it will help the curry cook faster and will give the curry its recognizable shine when served. Pour in your prepared sauce and the cooked meat and any juices that accumulated, pushing it right into the sauce. Cook for 10 minutes.

After 10 minutes, the sauce will be hot if you added oil and warm if you didn't. You will notice that the sauce has browned a little on top and possibly caramelized around the edges of the pan. That is flavour, so stir it in. Continue cooking for another 5 minutes or until the sauce is hot enough to serve.

Once the sauce is good and hot, stir in the yoghurt, kasoori methi and garam masala and push the quartered tomato deep into the sauce. Continue air frying for another 2–5 minutes to hear the tomato wedges through. Season with salt to taste and garnish with the chopped coriander (cilantro) and diced onion. You could also add a spoonful or more of Chilli raita, if you like.

# LAMB ACHARI
SERVES 1–2

Lamb achari is a curry made with pickling spices such as those you would expect to see in a jar of mango or lime pickle, like panch poran and dried chillies. It can be made spicy and savoury with lime pickle, or if you prefer it a bit sweet, you can also add mango chutney. Panch poran is Indian five spice and it's available at Indian grocers and online. If you have the whole spices, you can make it yourself by mixing equal amounts of cumin seeds, fenugreek seeds, black mustard seeds, fennel seeds and nigella seeds.

PREP TIME: 10 MINS
COOKING TIME: 30 MINS

300g (10½oz) Lamb tikka
    (see page 93)
Oil spray (optional)
2 tbsp natural yoghurt
½ tsp kasoori methi (dried
    fenugreek leaves)
½ tsp garam masala
Juice of 1 lemon or lime
2 tbsp finely chopped
    coriander (cilantro),
    to garnish
Salt, to taste

FOR THE SAUCE
2 medium onions, thinly sliced
½ red (bell) pepper, thinly
    sliced
1 tbsp rapeseed (canola) oil or
    oil spray
½ tsp salt
1 tbsp garlic and ginger paste
3 green finger chillies
1 tbsp curry powder or Mixed
    powder (see page 118)
½ tsp Kashmiri chilli powder
½ tsp ground cumin
½ tsp ground coriander
1½ tbsp paprika
5 cashews
125ml (½ cup) unseasoned
    passata
1 tbsp lime pickle or ½ tsp
    each lime pickle and
    mango chutney
250ml (1 cup) warm meat stock

FOR THE TEMPERING
2 tbsp rapeseed (canola) oil
1½ tsp panch poran
2 dried Kashmiri chillies
1 small red onion, thinly sliced

If you haven't already cooked the lamb tikka, do so now. Preheat the air fryer to 200°C (400°F). Spray the basket with oil and place the marinated or seasoned lamb inside to cook for about 15 minutes, turning once. When it's tender, transfer it to a plate. Set aside.

Place the onions, (bell) pepper, chillies, oil and salt into a mixing bowl. If you are on a reduced-calorie diet, squirt the veggies all over with oil spray instead of adding the oil. Mix it all up well. Pour it into the cooking basket and air fry for 10 minutes, stirring halfway through cooking. Carefully spread the garlic and ginger paste over the veggies for the last 2 minutes of cooking.

Pour it all back into the mixing bowl or a blender and add the remaining sauce ingredients. Blend with a stick blender or in the blender until smooth. Set aside.

Now pour the oil for tempering into a small cake tin or another suitable metal pan that fits inside your air fryer. Heat for 3 minutes and then add the panch poran and dried chillies. Fry for 1–2 minutes and then stir in the red onion and let this cook for 3 minutes or until the onion is soft. If you are on a reduced-calorie diet, you could spoon out some of the oil at this stage but it's better left in.

Pour in the blended sauce. Add the cooked lamb and any juices that accumulated and push it into the sauce. Cook for 10 minutes. After 10 minutes, the sauce will be getting hot. You will notice that the top of the sauce has darkened a little and you might see some caramelization around the sides of the pan. Stir this in for additional flavour. Continue cooking for another 5 minutes or until the sauce is hot enough to serve.

Stir in the yoghurt, kasoori methi and garam masala. Season with salt to taste and stir in the lemon or lime juice. Garnish with the chopped coriander (cilantro) to serve.

# KEEMA

SERVES 1–2

As popular as keema curries are, this one almost didn't make it into the book. I was having trouble air frying the keema until it was just right. Then about 3.30am one morning I awoke with this answer. Form the minced lamb into two burger patties and air fry them. Then finely chop the burgers. It worked, and this lamb keema recipe tastes just like those you find at good curry houses! If you have leftover burgers from your last barbecue, you could use them in the same way – this will cut the cooking time by 10 minutes and give you a nice smoky flavour.

PREP TIME: 10 MINS
COOKING TIME: 30 MINS

300g (10½oz) minced (ground) lamb or beef
Oil spray

FOR THE SAUCE
2 medium onions (approx. 250g/9oz), thinly sliced
½ red (bell) pepper, thinly sliced
1 tbsp rapeseed (canola) oil or oil spray
½ tsp salt
1 tbsp garlic and ginger paste
3 green finger chillies, sliced in half lengthwise
1 tbsp curry powder or Mixed powder (see page 118)
½ tsp Kashmiri chilli powder
½ tsp ground cumin
½ tsp ground coriander
1½ tbsp paprika
½ tsp ground turmeric
125ml (½ cup) unseasoned passata
250ml (1 cup) warm meat stock

TO FINISH
2 tbsp rapeseed (canola) oil (optional)
½ tsp kasoori methi (dried fenugreek leaves)
2.5cm (1in) piece of ginger, peeled and julienned
2 spring onions (scallions), thinly sliced
2 tbsp finely chopped coriander (cilantro)
Salt, to taste

Form the meat into two equal burger patties. Set your air fryer to 200°C (400°F) and spray the basket with oil. Place the burgers inside and spray the tops with oil too, then cook for 10 minutes or until cooked through. Transfer the cooked patties to a cutting board and go at them with a sharp knife. I spend a few minutes doing this as I like my keema really fine, but how much effort you put in is down to you. Set aside.

Place the onions, (bell) pepper, oil and salt in a mixing bowl. If you are on a reduced-calorie diet, squirt the veggies all over with oil spray instead of adding the oil. Mix it all up well. Pour it all into the cooking basket and air fry for 10 minutes, stirring halfway through cooking. Carefully spread the garlic and ginger paste over the veggies for the last 2 minutes of cooking.

Pour it all back into the mixing bowl or a blender and add the remaining sauce ingredients. Blend with a stick blender or in the blender until smooth. Set aside.

Pour the 2 tablespoons of oil into a small cake tin or another suitable metal pan that fits inside your air fryer. You could leave this step out and not add the oil but it will take a few minutes longer to cook the curry and it won't look as glossy. Heat it for a couple of minutes and then pour in the prepared sauce and keema. Cook for 10 minutes. After 10 minutes, you will notice that the top of the sauce has darkened a little and you might also see some sizzling caramelization around the edges of the pan. Stir this in for additional flavour. If you added oil to the pan, the curry should be quite hot, and if not it will be warm at this stage. Continue cooking for another 5 minutes or until the curry is hot enough to serve.

To finish, add the kasoori methi by rubbing it between your fingers over the curry. Stir this in and season with salt to taste. Garnish with the ginger, spring onions (scallions) and coriander (cilantro).

# BEEF BHUNA
SERVES 1–2

**Bhunas are normally thicker than other curry house-style curries. You want this to be thick enough that you can easily scoop it up with a naan or chapatti – that's how they are normally made. If you prefer more gravy, though, you could add a little more passata and/or stock and you will get just that. It won't be a 'bhuna' but it will still be an amazing curry to serve with rice. Curry house-style bhunas are bhunas in name only, as 'bhuna' is a style of cooking where small amounts of liquid are added to meat and other ingredients and slowly cooked until everything is tender. You don't have to go to such trouble with this one!**

PREP TIME: 10 MINS
COOKING TIME: 30 MINS

300g (10½oz) Beef tikka (see page 93) or cubed raw rump, rib-eye or sirloin
Oil spray (optional)

FOR THE SAUCE
2 medium onions (approx. 250g/9oz), thinly sliced
1 red (bell) pepper, thinly sliced
1 tbsp rapeseed (canola) oil or oil spray
½ tsp salt
1 tbsp garlic and ginger paste
1 tbsp curry powder, Mixed powder or Meat masala (see pages 118 and 119)
1 tsp tandoori masala
½ tsp ground turmeric
½ tsp Kashmiri chilli powder
1 tsp paprika
125ml (½ cup) unseasoned passata
70ml (¼ cup) warm meat stock

TO FINISH
2 tbsp rapeseed (canola) oil or oil spray
½ medium onion, finely chopped
2 tbsp finely chopped coriander (cilantro) stems, plus 2 tbsp finely chopped to garnish
½ tsp garam masala
½ tsp kasoori methi (dried fenugreek leaves)
1 generous tbsp natural yoghurt
Juice of 1 lemon or lime
1 spur chilli, thinly sliced
Salt, to taste

If you haven't already cooked the beef, do so now. Preheat the air fryer to 200°C (400°F). Spray the basket with oil to coat and place the beef pieces inside to cook for about 15 minutes or until tender, stirring once halfway through cooking. When the beef is good and tender, transfer it to a bowl and set aside.

Place the onions, (bell) pepper, oil and salt in a mixing bowl. If you are on a reduced-calorie diet, squirt the veggies all over with oil spray instead of adding the oil. Mix it all up well. Pour it all into the cooking basket and fry for 10 minutes, stirring halfway through cooking. Carefully spread the garlic and ginger paste over the veggies for the last 2 minutes of cooking.

Pour it all back into the mixing bowl or a blender and add the remaining sauce ingredients. Blend with a stick blender or in the blender until smooth. Set aside.

Pour the 2 tablespoons of oil, if using, into a small cake tin or another suitable metal pan that fits inside your air fryer. Set the cooking temperature to 200°C (400°F) and heat the oil for a couple of minutes. Add the chopped onions and coriander (cilantro) stems. If you didn't add the oil, spray the onions and stems to coat with cooking oil and air fry for 2 minutes or until the onion is turning soft. Pour in the blended sauce and add the cooked beef along with any juices that accumulated, pushing the meat right into the sauce. Cook for 10 minutes.

After 10 minutes, the sauce will begin to darken on the top and around the sides. Stir that in for additional flavour. If you used oil, the sauce will be hot and if you used spray, it will be warm. Give it all a good stir and continue air frying for another 5–10 minutes or until the curry is hot enough to serve.

Add the garam masala and kasoori methi. It's best to add the kasoori methi by rubbing it between your fingers over the curry. Whisk in the yoghurt and season with salt to taste, then squeeze in the citrus juice and stir well to combine.

To serve, garnish with the chopped coriander.

# LAMB ANDRAK

SERVES 1–2

Andrak means 'ginger' in Hindi and that is the dominant flavour in this curry. I didn't want to over-ginger you but I love the stuff and usually add more than this recipe calls for. I'll let you decide. This curry is medium spicy and I like to keep it that way so that the ginger is the star. Go ahead and add more chilli powder and/or chillies if you want a spicier curry.

**PREP TIME: 10 MINS**
**COOKING TIME: 30 MINS**

300g (10½oz) Lamb tikka (see page 93)
Oil spray (optional)

**FOR THE SAUCE**
2 medium onions (approx. 250g/9oz), thinly sliced
½ red (bell) pepper, cut in half and seeded
4 green finger chillies, sliced in half lengthwise
1 tbsp rapeseed (canola) oil or oil spray
½ tsp salt
1 tbsp garlic and ginger paste
1 tbsp curry powder or Mixed powder (see page 118)
½ tsp Kashmiri chilli powder
3 tbsp tomato purée (paste)
150ml (scant ⅔ cup) unseasoned passata
1 tbsp mango chutney
250ml (1 cup) warm meat stock

**FOR THE TEMPERING**
2 tbsp rapeseed (canola) oil
5cm (2in) cinnamon stick
Seeds from 4 green cardamom pods
1 star anise
1 small red onion, thinly sliced
7.5cm (3in) piece of ginger, peeled and julienned
½ red (bell) pepper, diced

**TO FINISH**
½ tsp garam masala
½ tsp kasoori methi (dried fenugreek leaves)
Juice of 1 lemon (optional)
2 tbsp finely chopped coriander (cilantro)
Salt, to taste

If you haven't already cooked the lamb tikka, do so now. Preheat the air fryer to 200°C (400°F). Spray the basket with oil and place the marinated or seasoned lamb inside to cook for about 15 minutes, turning once. When it's tender, transfer it to a plate. Set aside.

Place the onions, (bell) pepper, sliced chillies, the oil and the salt in a mixing bowl. If you are on a reduced-calorie diet, squirt the veggies all over with oil spray instead of adding the oil. Mix it all up well. Pour it all into the cooking basket and fry for 10 minutes, stirring halfway through cooking. Carefully spread the garlic and ginger paste over the veggies and cook for a further minute.

Take two of the sliced chillies (so four chilli slices) out of the sauce and set aside to garnish the curry later. Pour everything else back into the mixing bowl or a blender and add the remaining sauce ingredients. Blend with a stick blender or in the blender until smooth. Set aside.

Now pour the oil for tempering into a small cake tin or another suitable metal pan that fits inside your air fryer. Heat the oil at 200°C (400°C) for a couple of minutes and then add the cinnamon stick, cardamom seeds and star anise and fry for another minute or until it's bubbling hot and fragrant. Stir in the red onion, half of the julienned ginger and the (bell) pepper and air fry for about 3 minutes or until they are turning soft. If you are on a reduced-calorie diet, you could scoop out a lot of the oil and discard it. I don't!

Pour in your prepared sauce and the cooked lamb, along with any juices that accumulated. Push the lamb right down into the sauce and cook for 10 minutes. After 10 minutes, your sauce will be quite hot if you left the oil in and becoming warm if you removed it. The top of the sauce will have darkened a little and you might see some caramelization around the edges of the pan. Stir that in for additional flavour and continue cooking for 5 minutes or until the curry is hot enough to serve.

Add the garam masala and kasoori methi and season with salt to taste. Squeeze in the lemon juice if you like the citrusy flavour and garnish with the chopped coriander (cilantro), the remaining julienned ginger and the reserved halved chillies to serve.

# LAMB MADRAS

SERVES 1–2

**Madras curries are supposed to be spicy. Perhaps not as spicy as a vindaloo or phall but they should offer a good hot bite. You will get that with this recipe but it's not all about the heat. Together with the other warming spices and slightly sweetened with mango chutney, this curry is and probably always will be one of the most popular curry house-style curries.**

PREP TIME: 10 MINS
COOKING TIME: 30 MINS

300g (10½oz) lamb, cut into
    bite-sized pieces, or Lamb
    tikka (see page 93)
Oil spray (optional)
½ tsp garam masala
½ tsp kasoori methi (dried
    fenugreek leaves)
Juice of ½ lime
2 tbsp finely chopped coriander
    (cilantro), to garnish
Salt, to taste

FOR THE SAUCE

2 medium onions (approx.
    250g/9oz), thinly sliced
1 red (bell) pepper, cut in half
    and seeded
3 green finger chillies, chopped
1 tbsp rapeseed (canola) oil
    or oil spray
½ tsp salt
1 tbsp garlic and ginger paste
½ tsp ground turmeric
1 tbsp Mixed powder (see page
    118) or Madras curry powder
1 generous tbsp Kashmiri chilli
    powder (more or less to taste)
1 tbsp ground cumin
½ tsp ground coriander
1 tsp paprika
175ml (¾ cup) unseasoned
    passata
1 tbsp mango chutney or spicy
    lime pickle
250ml (1 cup) warm meat stock

FOR THE TEMPERING

2 tbsp rapeseed (canola) oil
2 dried red Kashmiri chillies
2 green cardamom pods, lightly
    crushed
3 green finger chillies, finely
    chopped

If you haven't already cooked the lamb, do so now. Preheat the air fryer to 200°C (400°F). Spray the basket with oil and place the marinated or seasoned lamb inside to cook for 15–20 minutes, turning once. When it's tender, transfer it to a plate. Set aside.

Place the onions, (bell) pepper, chillies, oil and salt in a mixing bowl. If you are on a reduced-calorie diet, squirt the veggies all over with oil spray instead of adding the oil. Mix it all up well. Pour it all into the cooking basket and fry for 10 minutes, stirring halfway through cooking. Carefully spread the garlic and ginger paste over the veggies for the last 2 minutes of cooking.

Pour it all back into the mixing bowl or a blender and add the remaining sauce ingredients. Blend with a stick blender or in the blender until smooth. Set aside.

Now pour the oil for tempering into a small cake tin or another suitable metal pan that fits inside your air fryer. Heat for 3 minutes and then add the dried chillies, cardamom pods and green chillies. Temper these in the hot oil for 1–2 minutes or until fragrant. If you are on a reduced-calorie diet, you could spoon out the majority of the oil at this stage but it's much better left in.

Pour the blended sauce into the pan. Add the cooked lamb and any juices that accumulated and air fry for 10 minutes. After 10 minutes, the sauce will be quite hot if you left the oil in and warm if not. You will notice that the top and edges of the sauce have browned and even caramelized around the edges. Stir that in for additional flavour. Continue cooking for another 5 minutes or until the curry is hot enough to serve.

To finish, season with salt to taste and stir in the garam masala. Add the kasoori methi by rubbing it between your fingers over the curry and then squeeze in the lime juice. Give it all another good stir and garnish with the chopped coriander (cilantro).

# SAAG PANEER

SERVES 1–2

**For this recipe, I suggest adding raw paneer and letting it heat through in the sauce. It's just an option, though, as you could also use tandoori-style paneer (see page 33), if you have some to hand or want to make that first. Whichever you decide to use, it is important that the paneer only be added to the pan for the last 5–7 minutes of cooking. You want it to be heated through, but if you cook it too long, it will begin to fall apart.**

PREP TIME: 10 MINS
COOKING TIME: 30 MINS

300g (10½oz) fresh baby
    spinach leaves, washed and
    patted dry
200g (7oz) mustard greens or
    more spinach
1 tbsp butter
1 tsp salt
200g (7oz) paneer, cut into
    2.5cm (1in) cubes
5 tbsp single (light) cream
    (more or less to taste)
½ tsp garam masala
Salt and pepper, to taste

FOR THE SAUCE

Oil spray
2 medium onions (approx.
    250g/9oz), thinly sliced
½ red (bell) pepper, cut in half
    and seeded
½ tsp salt
1 tbsp rapeseed (canola) oil
    (optional)
1 tbsp garlic and ginger paste
250ml (1 cup) warm vegetable
    stock

FOR THE TEMPERING

2 tbsp rapeseed (canola) oil
    or ghee
1 tsp cumin seeds
2 large garlic cloves,
    thinly sliced
2 green finger chillies,
    finely chopped
1 tsp chilli powder (more or
    less to taste)
1 tsp ground turmeric

Preheat the air fryer to 180°C (350°F). Add the greens and break the butter into small pieces and place it on top. Season with the salt and cook for 3 minutes. Stir well and continue cooking for another 2 minutes, then transfer to a bowl and set aside.

Increase the heat to 200°C (400°F) and spray the basket lightly with oil. Mix the onions, (bell) pepper and salt with the oil and place in the basket. If you are on a reduced-calorie diet, squirt the veggies all over with oil spray instead of adding the oil. Air fry for 10 minutes, stirring halfway through cooking. Carefully spread the garlic and ginger paste over these veggies for the last 2 minutes of cooking, then transfer to the bowl with the greens. Add the stock and blend until smooth, using a stick blender or a blender. Set aside.

Now pour the oil for tempering into a small cake tin or another suitable metal pan that fits inside your air fryer. Heat for 2 minutes, then add the cumin seeds, garlic and chopped chillies and air fry for 1–2 minutes or until fragrant. Be careful not to burn the garlic. Stir in the chilli powder and turmeric, then pour in the prepared sauce and continue cooking for 10 minutes.

After 10 minutes, the sauce will be quite hot because of the spice-infused oil. You will notice that the top of the sauce has darkened a little and you might see some caramelization around the edges of the pan. Give it a good stir and add the cubed paneer. Continue cooking for 5 minutes. Stir in the cream and garam masala and cook for another 2 minutes or until the curry is hot enough to serve. Season with salt and pepper to taste.

# BUTTER PANEER
SERVES 1–2

**This recipe is best prepared with the same marinated paneer used in the tandoori chicken legs on page 24. You can then add the reserved marinade to pimp up the sauce in this curry. You could also add raw paneer to the simmering sauce and let it heat through until soft. If doing this, add about 2 tablespoons of whisked yoghurt to the sauce at the end. The sauce should be very smooth – I run it through a fine sieve after blending, but that step is optional. If you substitute tandoori Chicken tikka and its marinade (see page 90) for the paneer, you will have yourself a delicious butter chicken.**

PREP TIME: 10 MINS
COOKING TIME: 15 MINS

250g (9oz) tandoori paneer (see page 33)
2 tbsp yoghurt, whisked, or all of the retained paneer marinade
3 tbsp single (light) cream
½ tsp garam masala
½ tsp kasoori methi (dried fenugreek leaves)
1 generous tbsp butter
Juice of ½ lemon
2 tbsp finely chopped coriander (cilantro), to garnish
Salt, to taste

FOR THE SAUCE
2 medium onions (approx. 250g/9oz), thinly sliced
1 red (bell) pepper, cut in half and seeded
1 tbsp rapeseed (canola) oil or oil spray
½ tsp salt
1 tbsp garlic and ginger paste
½ tsp ground turmeric
1 tbsp Madras curry powder or Mixed powder (see page 118)
1½ tsp Kashmiri chilli powder (more or less to taste)
½ tsp sugar, or to taste
250ml (1 cup) unseasoned passata
70ml (¼ cup) warm vegetable stock or water

FOR THE TEMPERING
2 tbsp rapeseed (canola) oil
2 green cardamom pods, lightly crushed
2 cloves
2.5cm (1in) cinnamon stick

Preheat the air fryer to 200°C (400°F). Place the onions, (bell) pepper, oil and the salt in a mixing bowl. If you are on a reduced-calorie diet, squirt the veggies all over with oil spray instead of adding the oil. Mix it all up well. Pour it all into the cooking basket and fry for 10 minutes, stirring halfway through cooking. Carefully spread the garlic and ginger paste over the veggies for the last 2 minutes of cooking.

Pour it all back into the mixing bowl or a blender and add the remaining sauce ingredients. Blend with a stick blender or in the blender until smooth. If you want the more traditional very smooth sauce, pass it all through a fine sieve. Set aside.

Now pour the oil for tempering into a small cake tin or another suitable metal pan that fits inside your air fryer. Heat for 3 minutes and then add the cardamom pods, cloves and cinnamon stick. Let these whole spices infuse into the oil for 1–2 minutes or until fragrant. If you don't like whole spices in your curries, fish them out. Otherwise, you can leave them in to continue flavouring the sauce. You can always remove them before serving. If you are on a reduced-calorie diet, you could spoon out some of the oil at this stage but it's much better left in.

Pour the blended sauce into the pan and air fry for 10 minutes. After 10 minutes, the sauce will be quite hot if you left the oil in. If not, it will be warm. At this stage you might see some caramelization around the edges of the sauce and a browned layer of sauce on the top. Stir that in for additional flavour. Add the paneer and let it heat through in the sauce for about 5 minutes.

If using tandoori paneer, stir in the marinade, or if cooking the paneer from raw, whisk in 2 tablespoons of yoghurt. Stir in the cream and garam masala and then add the kasoori methi by rubbing them between your fingers. Add the butter and continue cooking for 2 minutes or until the curry is hot enough to serve.

To finish, season with the lemon juice and salt to taste. Give it all another good stir and garnish with the chopped coriander (cilantro).

# ALOO GOBI

SERVES 1–2

**Aloo gobi is often served as a dry side or main dish. If that is what you are looking for, just leave out the sauce. This curry house version of aloo gobi includes a thick gravy, making it perfect for serving over rice. The key to success with this one is ensuring that the potatoes and cauliflower cook through at about the same time. You want to cut the potatoes as instructed below, and chop the cauliflower into florets slightly larger than the potato pieces.**

PREP TIME: 15 MINS
COOKING TIME: 40 MINS

1 floury potato (approx. 200g/7oz), cut into 2.5cm (1in) pieces
300g (10½oz) cauliflower florets, slightly larger than the potato pieces
½ medium red onion, divided into petals and then cut smaller to preference

FOR THE MARINADE
1 tbsp rapeseed (canola) oil or oil spray
1 tsp Kashmiri chilli powder
½ teaspoon amchoor (dried mango powder)
1 tsp ground coriander
½ tsp ground cumin
½ tsp ground turmeric
1 tbsp garlic and ginger paste
Salt, to taste
2 green finger chillies, thinly sliced (optional), to garnish

FOR THE SAUCE
2 medium onions (approx. 250g/9oz), thinly sliced
1 red (bell) pepper, cut in half and seeded
½ tsp salt
1 tbsp rapeseed (canola) oil or oil spray
1 tbsp garlic and ginger paste
½ tsp ground turmeric
1 tbsp Madras curry powder or Mixed powder (see page 118)
1½ tsp Kashmiri chilli powder (more or less to taste)
½ tsp sugar, or to taste
250ml (1 cup) unseasoned passata
70ml (¼ cup) vegetable stock or water

Place the potatoes, cauliflower and onion petals in a mixing bowl and add the marinade ingredients. Mix well to combine so that all the veggies are equally coated and set aside while you prepare the sauce.

Preheat the air fryer to 200°C (400°F). Place the onions, (bell) pepper and salt in a mixing bowl and add the oil. If you are on a reduced-calorie diet, squirt the veggies all over with oil spray instead of adding the oil. Mix well and then pour it all into the basket of your air fryer. Air fry for 10 minutes, stirring or shaking the basket halfway through cooking. Add the garlic and ginger paste for the last 2 minutes of cooking.

Pour it all back into the mixing bowl or a blender and add the remaining sauce ingredients. Blend with a stick blender or in the blender until smooth. Set aside.

Now spray the air fryer basket with oil and add the marinated cauliflower, onion petals and potatoes. Air fry at 200°C (400°F) for 10 minutes, shaking the basket once halfway through cooking for a more even cook. After 10 minutes, check the cauliflower and potatoes for doneness and continue cooking until cooked to your liking. Transfer to a bowl and set aside.

Pour the blended sauce into a small cake tin or another suitable metal pan that fits inside your air fryer. Air fry for 10 minutes. After 10 minutes, the top and sides will have darkened some, and that is flavour so stir it in. Add the cooked cauliflower, potatoes and onion petals and stir them into the sauce. Continue air frying for 5–10 minutes or until the curry is hot enough to serve. Season with salt to taste and garnish with the thinly sliced chillies if you want a bit more heat.

NOTE
If you heat 2 tablespoons of oil in your pan for a couple of minutes before adding the blended sauce, it will cook faster and, in my opinion, look and taste better too.

# RAJMA

SERVES 1–2

As vegetarian curries go, rajma, or kidney bean curry, is one of the most popular. This simple recipe will get you restaurant quality results. Here, you use tinned (canned) kidney beans for ease. You could, of course, soak and cook dried kidney beans if you would like to – I actually prefer using dried, as you can add some of the soaking cooking liquid to the curry as well, but that is sometimes one step too many when I just want to cook up a quick rajma.

**PREP TIME: 10 MINS**
**COOKING TIME: 20 MINS**

1–2 tbsp rapeseed (canola) oil (optional)
600g (1lb 5oz) tinned (canned) kidney beans, strained
½ tsp kasoori methi (dried fenugreek leaves)
½ tsp garam masala
Salt, to taste
3 tbsp finely chopped coriander (cilantro), to garnish

**FOR THE SAUCE**
2 medium onions (approx. 250g/9oz), thinly sliced
1 red or orange (bell) pepper, cut in half and seeded
1 tbsp rapeseed (canola) oil or oil spray
½ tsp salt
1 tbsp garlic and ginger paste
2 green finger chillies
70ml (¼ cup) unseasoned passata
125ml (½ cup) vegetable stock
½ tsp Kashmiri chilli powder (more or less to taste)
½ tsp ground turmeric
1½ tsp ground cumin
1½ tsp ground coriander

Preheat the air fryer to 200°C (400°F). Place the onions, (bell) pepper, oil and salt in a mixing bowl. If you are on a reduced-calorie diet, squirt the veggies all over with oil spray instead of adding the oil. Mix it all up well. Pour it all into the cooking basket and fry for 10 minutes, stirring halfway through cooking. Carefully spread the garlic and ginger paste over the veggies for the last 2 minutes of cooking.

Pour it all back into the mixing bowl or a blender and add the remaining sauce ingredients. Blend with a stick blender or in the blender until smooth. Set aside.

Pour the oil, if using, into a small cake tin or another suitable metal pan that fits inside your air fryer. Heat the oil for a couple of minutes, if using, and then pour in the smooth sauce and cook for 10 minutes. The sauce will begin to brown on top and around the sides. It will be quite hot if you used oil and warm if you didn't.

Add the kidney beans and stir them in. Continue air frying for another 5–10 minutes or until the curry is hot enough to serve.

To finish, add the kasoori methi by rubbing it between your fingers over the curry. Add the garam masala and season with salt to taste. Give it all another good stir and garnish with the chopped coriander (cilantro).

# TANDOORI FAVOURITES

You are going to love how close to authentic tandoori dishes these recipes taste cooked in a simple air fryer! You will find all the most popular tandoori recipes in this chapter. Air fryers are ideal for cooking tandoori food because they offer an intense heat with lots of air circulation.

In this section you will also learn how to give the dishes a smoky flavour, as if they were cooked in a charcoal-burning tandoor, using a traditional Indian smoking technique called the dhungar method.

## THE DHUNGAR METHOD OF SMOKING

To give tandoori air fried dishes a smoky flavour and simulate cooking in a charcoal-burning tandoor, try the following technique:

Prepare your marinade and rub it into whatever you are cooking. Light one or two pieces of lumpwood charcoal that have not been coated with lighter fuel, as this will give a bad flavour when smoking. When hot and burning, place them on a piece of two-ply foil or even in a small metal saucer. For additional flavour, you could also add a few cardamom pods and cloves and/or a small cinnamon stick to the burning charcoal.

If marinating small pieces of meat, move the meat to the sides of your mixing bowl, leaving a small recess in the centre. Place the burning charcoal in the centre. To marinate a large joint of meat, such as a whole chicken, place it in a large bowl with all the marinade, leaving space to place the burning charcoal next to it.

Drizzle a few drops of oil over the burning charcoal. It will be very smoky, fast. Cover it all tightly with a glass lid. You want to use a glass lid so that you can see what is happening inside. As the lid cuts off the oxygen, the fire will go out and it will stop smoking. This whole process takes about 15 minutes.

You don't want to leave it until all the smoke is gone, but rather until about 95 per cent of it is and you can see the marinating meat, fish or paneer clearly through the lid. Remove the lid and charcoal and continue marinating, covered in the fridge, or go straight to cooking. Longer marination time will usually have its flavour benefits but please always refer to the recipe.

This traditional smoking technique will give a delicious smoky flavour to any of the following tandoori recipes and can also be used to give a smoky flavour to a curry.

## USING YOUR AIR FRYER AS A TANDOOR OVEN

The recipes in this section are all recipes that are often cooked in tandoor ovens at restaurants. The recipes work because air fryers offer the air flow and heat required to cook tandoori dishes. The great thing is, air fryers don't only cook tandoori food well but they are easier to use and heat up a lot quicker too.

**Are there other ways of getting a smoky flavour using an air fryer?**

At the time of writing and to my knowledge, only Ninja produce a range of outdoor air fryer smokers. I've heard they're quite good and work the same way as Traeger and other wood pellet barbecues for smoking but with the added air fryer.

**Is smoking your tandoori dishes necessary?**

Not at all. Most restaurant tandoor ovens are gas fuelled nowadays so any smokiness you taste is due to the juices hitting the gas heated coals at the bottom of the oven and smoking when they do. That said, you might like to try using the dhungar method to smoke your food as it marinates. It is worth noting that you can also use the same technique to add a smoky flavour to a curry, which will make it taste as if it were cooked slowly over fire. To do so, make a recess in the centre of your curry and smoke it in the same way as you smoke marinating meat, seafood and paneer, described opposite.

# CHICKEN TIKKA

SERVES 4

**This chicken tikka recipe is delicious served on its own with a few dips or added to a chicken curry. If serving as a starter, you might like to skewer them with wooden skewers for better presentation. Just be sure to soak the wooden skewers for about 30 minutes before air frying or they could burn. The chicken tikka is delicious served in any curry in this book so I often make more than I need for a recipe and freeze the rest for later. It freezes really well and speeds up the cooking process for the different curries. You will also get another layer of amazing flavour compared to cooking unmarinated chicken.**

PREP TIME: 20 MINS,
    PLUS MARINATING
COOKING TIME: 20 MINS

600g (1lb 5oz) skinless chicken
    breasts or thighs, cut into
    bite-sized tikka
Oil spray
2 tbsp melted ghee (optional)
Lime wedges, to serve

FOR THE FIRST MARINADE
Juice of 2 lemons
2 tbsp garlic and ginger paste
1 tbsp mustard oil or rapeseed
    (canola) oil (optional; I use
    mustard oil)
Salt, to taste

FOR THE SECOND
    MARINADE
1 tbsp Kashmiri chilli powder
    (more or less to taste)
1 tbsp ground cumin
2 tsp ground coriander
2 tsp tandoori masala
210ml (1 cup) Greek yoghurt

Place the chicken pieces in a large mixing bowl and add the lemon juice, some salt, the garlic and ginger paste and the oil, if using. Mix this right into the flesh of the chicken pieces and set aside while you prepare the second marinade or for up to 2 hours.

To make the second marinade, whisk all the ingredients together and pour the marinade over the chicken. Again, rub this right into the flesh so that the chicken is completely coated. Allow to marinate for at least 30 minutes or overnight. Now is a good time to check out the dhungar method of smoking on page 89 if you are interested.

When ready to cook, preheat the air fryer to 200°C (400°F) and spray the basket with oil. Remove any excess marinade and then skewer the chicken onto wooden skewers, if you like, and place in the basket. Spray the top of the meat with oil to coat. Air fry for 15–20 minutes, turning the skewers halfway through cooking. Towards the end of cooking, baste the chicken with the ghee, if using, a couple of times. When your chicken tikka is cooked through and you are happy with the char on the exterior, transfer to a serving plate.

Season with salt to taste if needed and serve immediately, with lime wedges to squeeze over, or save to add to a curry.

# MEAT TIKKA WITH CUCUMBER RAITA

SERVES 4

**Lamb and beef tikka are quick, easy and, most importantly, delicious when done this way. The meat can be used in a curry house-style curry or served as a starter with a good raita or chutney. The optional cucumber raita here is a good one. The meat tikka is also nice wrapped in homemade naans with salad vegetables and hot sauce. If you like a good lamb or beef curry, you might like to upscale this recipe to make more so that you have it when needed. Having cooked and tender tandoori meat on hand is a real timesaver. The cooked tandoori meat freezes well for up to 6 months in an air-tight container.**

PREP TIME: 10 MINS,
  PLUS MARINATING
COOKING TIME: 10 MINS

800g (1lb 12oz) lamb leg meat, trimmed of fat and cut into cubes, or the same weight of beef rump, ribeye or sirloin
Oil spray

FOR THE FIRST MARINADE
2 tbsp Garlic, ginger and chilli paste (see page 120)
½ tsp salt (or to taste)
Juice of 2 limes

FOR THE SECOND MARINADE
1 tbsp garam masala
1 tsp chilli powder
1 tbsp ground cumin
1 tsp ground coriander
1 tsp kasoori methi (dried fenugreek leaves)
1 tbsp mustard oil or rapeseed (canola) oil
1 tsp English mustard
1 tbsp mint sauce

FOR THE RAITA
500ml (2 cups) Greek yoghurt
½ tsp ground cumin
2 garlic cloves, minced
½ English cucumber, peeled and seeded
4 tbsp finely chopped coriander (cilantro)
1 tsp lime juice
Salt and pepper, to taste

Place the meat in a large mixing bowl and add the garlic, ginger and chilli paste, salt and lime juice. Rub this marinade right into the meat and let it marinate while you prepare the second marinade or for up to 3 hours.

To make the second marinade, whisk all the ingredients together until smooth. Pour this over the meat and stir well to combine so that the meat is evenly coated with the marinade. For best results, let the meat marinate for at least 30 minutes or up to 72 hours. The longer, the better, but you could go straight to cooking if you are in a rush.

When ready to cook, preheat the air fryer to 200°C (400°F) and spray the basket with oil. Rub off any excess marinade and place the meat directly in your air fryer basket, spraying the top of the meat with oil.

Air fry for 15–20 minutes or until the meat is nicely charred on the exterior and juicy and tender inside. Turn the meat halfway through cooking for an even cook. Season with more salt to taste and serve hot or use in a curry.

TO MAKE THE RAITA

Place the yoghurt in a mixing bowl and whisk until smooth. Whisk in the cumin and garlic and set aside. Finely dice the cucumber and squeeze out any excess water. Add the diced cucumber to the yoghurt and stir it in.

Now add the coriander (cilantro) and lime juice. Season with salt and pepper to taste. Raitas are best served chilled, so place the finished cucumber raita in the fridge until ready to serve.

# EASY WHOLE TANDOORI CHICKEN
SERVES 3–4

Tandoor ovens are great for cooking whole chicken but not many people have one. They are also difficult to use if you're new to them. Air fryers make the process of cooking tandoori chicken so much easier, with very similar results. Your air fryer is nothing more than a small but efficient oven. The way the air flows simulates the radiating heat from the tandoor walls. If you want a smokier flavour, try using the dhungar method explained on page 89. It works wonders! I leave the chicken skin on for this recipe but you could remove it and score the meat in about 12 places as in the recipe overleaf, which is a more traditional way of preparing a chicken for tandoori cooking.

PREP TIME: 20 MINS,
PLUS MARINATING
COOKING TIME: 50 MINS

1.5kg (3lb 5oz) whole chicken
70ml (¼ cup) melted ghee
  mixed with 1 tsp salt
Red onion chutney (see page
  14) or other sauce of your
  choice, to serve (optional)

FOR THE TANDOORI
  MARINADE
1 tbsp ground cumin
1 tbsp ground coriander
1 tbsp tandoori masala
1 tbsp garam masala
1 tsp ground turmeric
1 tsp amchoor (dried mango
  powder – optional)
1 tbsp Kashmiri chilli powder
  (more or less to taste), or
  mild paprika)
2 tbsp Garlic, ginger and
  chilli paste (see page 120)
1 tsp freshly ground
  black pepper
1 tsp salt
3 tbsp lemon juice
1 tbsp distilled white vinegar
4 tbsp rapeseed (canola) oil
4 tbsp Greek yoghurt, whisked
  until smooth (optional)
Red food colouring powder
  (optional)

Whisk together all the marinade ingredients, adding just enough water to make a smooth paste – about 3 tablespoons. I use a little red food colouring, too, but it adds no flavour so it is optional.

Rub the marinade all over the chicken, including inside the carcass and underneath the skin if you like to add more flavour. Cover and leave to marinate in the fridge for 1–4 hours. If you add yoghurt, you can leave it to marinate for up to 24 hours.

When ready to cook, preheat the air fryer to 180°C/350°F. Place the chicken in the air fryer basket, breast-side down. Cook for 50 minutes. Baste the chicken from time to time with the melted ghee.

After 50 minutes of air frying, flip the chicken over with a pair of tongs and baste it with the ghee. Continue cooking for a further 10–15 minutes to make the skin nice and crispy. Make sure the internal temperature of the chicken is 74°C/165°F before removing from your air fryer.

Allow the chicken to rest for 5–8 minutes before carving. In the photo the chicken is served with the red onion chutney from page 14 but you can serve it with your raita, chutney or sauce of choice.

# SOUTHERN-STYLE TANDOORI CHICKEN

SERVES 3–4

South Indian recipes are becoming very popular at curry houses these days. This is a simple chicken recipe with few ingredients but the marinade flavours go so well together and taste amazing on the roasted chicken. This recipe would work equally well with smaller cuts like chicken legs or chicken tikka, though you will need to watch it and adjust the cooking time. Remember the chicken is cooked when it reaches an internal temperature of 74°C/165°F.

PREP TIME: 20 MINS, PLUS
  MARINATING
COOKING TIME: 50 MINS

1.5kg (3lb 5oz) whole chicken,
  skin removed
Oil spray

FOR THE FIRST MARINADE
70ml (¼ cup) lime juice
1 tsp salt
4 tbsp Garlic, ginger and
  chilli paste (see page 120)
30 fresh or frozen curry leaves,
  finely chopped
1 tbsp freshly ground
  black pepper
1 tbsp rapeseed (canola) oil
  (optional)

FOR THE SECOND
  MARINADE
½ tsp cumin seeds, preferably
  roasted (see page 118)
3 tbsp coriander seeds,
  preferably roasted
  (see page 118)
210ml (1 cup) Greek yoghurt
200ml (¾ cup) thick
  coconut milk
½ tsp salt

Score the chicken all over the breasts and thighs and set aside. In a mixing bowl, whisk all the first marinade ingredients until smooth and then rub the marinade right into the flesh of the chicken and inside the cavity. Cover and allow to marinate in the fridge for 10–20 minutes while you prepare the second marinade.

To make the second marinade, grind the cumin and coriander seeds into a powder and then whisk it into the yoghurt and coconut milk with the salt. Rub this all over and inside the chicken and allow to marinate, covered in the fridge, for 30 minutes or up to 48 hours. The longer, the better. If in a real rush, you could go straight to cooking but that marination time does have flavour benefits!

When ready to cook, preheat your air fryer to 180°C/350°F and spray the basket with oil to coat. Rub all the excess marinade off the chicken and place it in the air fryer basket, breast-side down. Retain the excess marinade for basting. Cook for 30 minutes and then turn the chicken over. Baste lightly with some of the excess marinade and spray with oil to coat the top.

Continue cooking for 20–30 minutes or until cooked through. Make sure the internal temperature is 74°C/165°F before removing from your air fryer. Allow the chicken to rest for 5–8 minutes before carving. This is delicious served with coriander and chilli chutney, or with the masala fries on page 112.

# TANDOORI LAMB CHOPS WITH CORIANDER CHUTNEY

SERVES 2–3

**These tandoori lamb chops taste just like they were cooked in a charcoal-burning tandoor. In my opinion, these are so much better when they have been smoked using the dhungar method, so I have included the method on page 89 here, but that is optional. Just leave it out if you want. Even if you don't smoke the lamb, you are certain to love this dish, as the marinade is just like those I learned at so many restaurants and food stalls over the years.**

PREP TIME: 5 MINS,
PLUS MARINATING
COOKING TIME: 12 MINS

1 tbsp rapeseed (canola) oil, plus 1 tbsp for smoking (optional(
½ tsp salt
½ tsp freshly ground black pepper
3 tbsp Garlic, ginger and chilli paste (see page 120)
1 tbsp garam masala
½ tsp ground turmeric
1 tbsp Kashmiri chilli powder
Juice of 1 lemon
6 lamb chops on the bone, excess surface fat removed
100ml (½ cup) Greek yoghurt
Oil spray
1 tbsp melted ghee, for basting, (optional)
2 tbsp finely chopped coriander (cilantro), to garnish

FOR THE CORIANDER CHUTNEY

1 tsp roasted cumin seeds (see page 118)
1 large bunch of coriander (cilantro)
3 green chillies
2 garlic cloves
Juice of 1 lemon
Salt, to taste

In a large bowl, mix the oil, salt, pepper, garlic, ginger and chilli paste, garam masala, turmeric, chilli powder and lemon juice together. Add the lamb chops and massage the marinade into the meat. Let this stand for about 20 minutes. Rub the yoghurt into the meat and let it marinate for at least 30 minutes or up to 72 hours. The longer, the better. If you are marinating the meat for longer than 1 hour, be sure to cover it tightly with cling film (plastic wrap) or store it in a plastic freezer bag in the fridge.

Now it's time to smoke the meat. If not doing this, jump to the next paragraph. Make a recess in the centre of the marinating lamb chops and place one or two pieces of burning charcoal on a two-ply piece of foil in the centre. You can add spices like cinnamon, cardamom pods and cloves to the charcoal for more flavour if you like. Drizzle 1 teaspoon of the oil over the burning charcoal and it will begin to smoke like crazy. Quickly cover the bowl and let it smoke until almost all the smoke is gone, which will take about 20 minutes. A glass lid will come in handy so that you can see the progress. Once most of the smoke has subsided, remove the charcoal and put someplace safe. You can do this at any time while the lamb marinates.

When ready to cook, preheat the air fryer to 200°C (400°F). Spray the basket with oil, place the lamb chops inside and air fry for 15–20 minutes, turning and basting with the ghee, if using, at least once during cooking. When nicely charred and cooked to your liking, remove from the heat and leave to rest for about 5 minutes. At Indian restaurants, lamb chops are usually cooked until well done but that doesn't mean you have to do that. The internal cooked temperature of lamb chops is 55°C/131°F for medium rare, 60°C/140°F for medium, 65°C/149°F for medium well and 72°C/162°F for well done.

Season with salt and pepper and serve garnished with coriander (cilantro).

FOR THE CORIANDER CHUTNEY
Blend all the chutney ingredients until you have a smooth chutney. That's it... your work is done. Enjoy!

# CHEESE-FILLED KOFTAS WITH CHILLI RAITA

SERVES 2–3

**This recipe calls for roasted gram flour, which is optional but gives the koftas a delicious nutty flavour. You can purchase roasted gram flour or make your own by toasting normal gram flour in a dry pan until fragrant and a couple of tones darker. It only takes a couple of minutes but if you don't want to use another pan, just use unroasted gram flour. These koftas are a real treat and can be made with beef or lamb. Bite into them and the cheesy filling takes the standard kofta and turns it into a masterpiece.**

PREP TIME: 10 MINS,
   PLUS MARINATING
   (OPTIONAL)
COOKING TIME: 15 MINS

1 tbsp cumin seeds
1 tbsp coriander seeds
500g (1lb 2oz) minced (ground)
   beef or lamb
2 tbsp garlic and ginger paste
2 tsp Kashmiri chilli powder
1 tsp garam masala
1 tsp ground cumin
½ red onion, very finely
   chopped
3 tbsp finely chopped
   coriander (cilantro) stems
3 green finger chillies,
   finely chopped
1 tbsp roasted gram flour
   (optional)
150g (5½oz) Cheddar or
   mozzarella cheese, grated
Oil spray
2 tbsp melted ghee (optional)
Salt and pepper, to taste
2 lemons, quartered, to serve

FOR THE CHILLI RAITA
500ml (2 cups) natural yoghurt
Juice of 1 lime
1 tsp red chilli powder (more or
   less, to taste)
Chaat masala and/or salt,
   to taste

Using a pestle and mortar or spice grinder, coarsely grind the cumin and coriander seeds. This should not be a powder. Pour the ground spices into a mixing bowl and add the remaining ingredients up to and including the gram flour. Mix well to combine with your hands, kneading it all so that you break down the meat until smooth. This should take a couple of minutes. You can leave this to marinate for up to 48 hours or go straight to cooking. Allowing it all to marinate does have its flavour benefits. If you are marinating the meat for longer than 1 hour, be sure to cover it tightly with cling film (plastic wrap) or store it in a plastic freezer bag in the fridge.

When ready to cook, divide the meat mixture into eight equal round koftas. Place a bowl of water next to you. Take one of the koftas and press your thumb into it and then fill it with some of the cheese. Bring the meat around the cheese and then, with wet hands, roll it into a neat ball. Repeat with the remaining meat and cheese.

Preheat the air fryer to 200°C (400°F). Spray the basket with oil to coat and place the koftas inside. Spray the tops of the koftas with oil and cook for 15 minutes, turning and spraying again with oil halfway through cooking. A delicious alternative to spraying the koftas with oil is to brush them with melted ghee at the start of cooking and then basting them one or two more times during cooking with the ghee.

For the chilli raita, place all the ingredients in a mixing bowl. Whisk until creamy smooth and keep it in the fridge until required.

Serve the koftas hot with lemon wedges and the chilli raita. The lemon juice can be squeezed over the koftas to taste at the table. These koftas are also good served with a coriander chutney (see page 121).

# TANDOORI PRAWNS

SERVES 2–4

**You can use any size of prawns for this recipe, but I like to use large jumbo prawns. You will need to adjust the cooking times if using smaller prawns but that's easy when using an air fryer. Just keep checking on them and remove when cooked to your liking.**

PREP TIME: 10 MINS,
  PLUS MARINATING
  (OPTIONAL)
COOKING TIME: 10 MINS

500g (1lb 2oz) king prawns
  (jumbo shrimp), peeled and
  deveined with tails intact
8 cherry or baby plum
  tomatoes
8 green chillies
Hot sauce, chapattis and salad
  vegetables of your choice,
  to serve (optional)

FOR THE FIRST MARINADE
1 tbsp rapeseed (canola) oil or
  oil spray
1 tbsp garlic and ginger paste
¼ tsp ground turmeric
1 tsp salt
½ tsp finely ground
  white pepper

FOR THE SECOND
  MARINADE
3 tbsp Greek yoghurt
1 tbsp single (light) cream
1 tbsp garlic and ginger paste
1 green finger chilli, finely
  chopped
1 tbsp chopped coriander
  (cilantro)
1 tsp salt
½ tsp ajwain (carom) seeds
1 tsp Kashmiri chilli powder

Place the prawns, tomatoes and chillies in a dish, mix in all the ingredients for the first marinade and set aside while you prepare the second marinade or for up to 20 minutes. If you are on a reduced-calorie diet, you can omit the oil and spray these ingredients to coat with oil spray.

Mix together all the ingredients for the second marinade and massage them into the prawns. You can let the prawns marinate for another 20 minutes or go straight to cooking. Thread the prawns, tomatoes and chillies onto six wooden skewers that have been soaked in water for 30 minutes.

Preheat the air fryer to 200°C (400°F) and cook for 8 minutes or until the prawns begin to char in places and are cooked through. Serve hot on their own or with a good hot sauce, chapattis and your preferred salad vegetables.

# TANDOORI SEA BREAM
SERVES 2

**When I first started cooking in my tandoor, I lost a lot of fish into the coals before learning how to skewer them correctly. With this recipe, you don't have to worry about such things as the fish cooks perfectly in the air fryer. It really is just like the fish I cook in my tandoor, without all the fuss!**

PREP TIME: 10 MINS
COOKING TIME: 20 MINS

2 x 250g (9oz) sea bream or
  other fish of your choice
2–3 lemons, 1 thinly sliced
  (optional), plus 2, quartered,
  to serve
Oil spray
Salt and pepper, to taste

FOR THE MARINADE
3 tbsp Greek yoghurt
1 tsp rapeseed (canola) oil
Juice of 1 lemon
2 garlic cloves, finely chopped
2cm (¾in) piece of ginger,
  finely chopped
2 green finger chillies, finely
  chopped or smashed into
  a paste
1 tbsp tandoori masala

Place all the marinade ingredients in a bowl and whisk until creamy and smooth. I like slightly larger chunks of garlic in the marinade, as they do char nicely, but you could mince the garlic if you prefer. Set aside.

To prepare the fish, take a sharp knife and scrape it down the skin a few times on both sides. This is important as you want to scrape as much excess moisture from the skin as possible. As you scrape the skin, you will see how much moisture is scraped off. The skin needs to feel dry.

Score the skin a few times on both sides and season with salt and pepper to taste. Then open the cavity and season it generously with salt and pepper too. Apply a thin layer of the marinade inside the cavity. If you like, you can also add a few slices of lemon too.

Spray the air fryer basket with oil and preheat the air fryer to 200°C (400°F). Place the fish in the basket and cook for 10 minutes. Then brush the fish lightly with marinade. Carefully turn the fish over and brush the other side with marinade and allow to cook for another 10 minutes or until cooked through. You can easily check that the fish is cooked by opening the cavity and looking at the meat. It is cooked when the meat between the head and body has turned from opaque to white in colour and is a bit flaky.

Turn the fish once more and cook for another 3–5 minutes. Using a metal spatula, carefully and gently lift the fish out of the cooking basket. Serve immediately with lemon wedges that can be squeezed over the fish at the table.

# STUFFED MUSHROOMS
SERVES 2–4

This is a recipe I learned while in Jaipur and decided it needed to be in this book. Although the filling is normally fried in a pan, it works really well in an air fryer. When I made it there, the stuffed mushrooms were then cooked in a tandoor. You can easily work ahead and make the stuffing and fill the mushrooms. Then just heat up the stuffed mushrooms up for about 10 minutes in your air fryer and enjoy.

**PREP TIME: 15 MINS**
**COOKING TIME: 25 MINS**

10 large chestnut (cremini) mushrooms
1 small red onion, very finely chopped
2 green finger chillies, finely chopped
10 curry leaves, finely chopped
1½ tbsp garlic and ginger paste
1–2 tbsp rapeseed (canola) oil (optional) or oil spray
1 egg
2 tbsp cream cheese
4 tbsp grated paneer or Cheddar or any cheese you like
4 tbsp panko breadcrumbs
2 tbsp finely chopped coriander (cilantro)
½ tsp kasoori methi (dried fenugreek leaves)
Coriander chutney (see page 99), to serve
Salt and pepper, to taste

Carefully remove the stems from the mushrooms. Retain the stems. Use a spoon to scoop out any remnants of the stems left behind so that you have as large a space as possible for stuffing the mushrooms. Chop the stems very finely and place in a mixing bowl. Add the onion, chillies, curry leaves and garlic and ginger paste.

Preheat the air fryer to 200°C (400°F). Pour 1–2 tablespoons of oil into a small cake tin or other metal pan that fits into your air fryer and place it inside the cooking basket for 2 minutes. If you are on a reduced-calorie diet, you can just generously coat the veggies with oil spray instead. Add the contents of the mixing bowl and stir them into the oil. Cook, stirring once or twice, for 10 minutes or until the mushroom stems, onion and chillies are soft. Transfer to a bowl and allow to cool.

In another bowl, whisk the egg and cream cheese together until smooth and set aside. Once the stuffing mixture has cooled, add the grated cheese, the panko breadcrumbs and coriander (cilantro). Season it all generously with salt and pepper and add the kasoori methi leaves by rubbing them between your fingers over it all. Stir in the egg and cream cheese mixture to bind the stuffing together.

Fill the recesses of the mushrooms with the stuffing, getting as much as you can into each mushroom. Spray your cooking basket with oil, place the stuffed mushrooms in the basket and air fry for 10–15 minutes. Be sure to check the mushrooms often and remove when heated through and nicely browned on top.

Transfer to a plate covered with paper towel just before serving. Mushrooms contain a lot of water, which will be soaked up by the paper towels. Serve immediately with coriander chutney or your choice of sauce.

# BASICS AND SIDE DISHES

When you make one or more of the main dishes in this book, you will no doubt want a few good side dishes to go with them. These recipes have been tried and tested many times so that they are as good as they can possibly be. Remember those air fryer cooking limitations I mentioned at the beginning of the book. You can decide whether to cook some of these in more traditional ways or give them a go in your air fryer. I have highlighted any potential issues where necessary.

# PERFECT AIR FRYER BASMATI RICE

SERVES 2

**You might wonder why you would want to cook rice in an air fryer as more traditional methods are easy and get great results. This recipe is just a bit of fun and it gets great results too!**

**Just like the fluffy basmati rice recipe in my previous books, this air fryer version uses the absorption method for perfect rice every time. When cooking rice, you want to ensure that the metal cooking vessel you use can hold all the rice, and that the rice only fills it by one third at most, so the rice has room to expand when cooking.**

PREP TIME: 5 MINS,
PLUS SOAKING
COOKING TIME: 35 MINS

185g (1 cup) basmati rice
500ml (2 cups) boiling water
1 tbsp butter or ghee (optional)
½ tsp salt

Pour the rice into a mixing bowl and run it under your tap to cover. Swirl the rice around in the water with your hand. The water will become milky from the starch. Pour the water out and repeat five times or until the water is almost clear. Then pour out the water and cover the rice with fresh water to soak for at least 30 minutes or up to a few hours if more convenient.

Preheat the air fryer to 200°C (400°F). Strain the rice and pour it into a small cake tin or metal pan that fits inside the cooking chamber. Cover with the boiling water and add the butter, if using, and salt. Cover tightly with foil and air fry for 30 minutes. After 30 minutes, let the rice sit for 5 minutes and then remove it from the air fryer and take off the foil.

Fluff the rice with a fork or chopstick. It is important to delicately fluff the rice so take some time to do this. Do not stir vigorously or the rice will split and become mushy.

# FRIED PILAU RICE

SERVES 2

**All you need is cooked rice before starting this recipe. You could use the air fryer method opposite or just cook the rice as you like. I have given my saucepan-steamed recipe below. The cooking time does not include the initial rice cooking time as this recipe is perfect for using up leftovers.**

PREP TIME: 10 MINS
COOKING TIME: 20 MINS

FOR THE RICE
185g (1 cup) basmati rice (or leftover, cold cooked rice)
½ tsp salt

TO FINISH
2 tbsp ghee
3 green cardamom pods
5cm (2in) cinnamon stick, lightly crushed
½ tsp cumin seeds
½ tsp cloves
½ tsp black peppercorns
1 Indian bay leaf (cassia leaf – optional)
½ onion, finely chopped
½ tsp salt
½ tsp ground turmeric
1 tbsp finely chopped coriander (cilantro)

Cooking the rice is easy in an air fryer (see opposite) but if you would rather use the pan method, I have that for you here. If you already have cold, cooked basmati rice, you can jump to the third paragraph. Pour the rice into a bowl and cover with water. With your hand, move the rice around in the water. The water will become milky from the starch. Repeat five times and then cover with fresh water to soak for at least 30 minutes.

Once your rice has soaked, pour it through a sieve and then pour all the rice into a saucepan with a tight-fitting lid. With this method, the rice to water ratio is always 1 part rice to 1½ parts water so add 500ml (2 cups) water, cover with a lid and bring the water to the boil. Once boiling, turn off the heat and leave to steam for 40 minutes without disturbing. After 40 minutes, lightly stir the rice with a fork or chopstick to separate the grains and place in the fridge to cool or use immediately in this recipe.

Preheat the air fryer to 200°C (400°F). Place a metal cake tin or another suitable metal pan with the ghee in your air fryer and heat it for 3 minutes. Stir in the cardamom pods, cinnamon stick, cumin seeds, cloves, black peppercorns and bay leaf, if using, and fry for 3 minutes. Then add the onion and salt and continue frying for 5 minutes or until soft and translucent. Stir in the ground turmeric until the onion is yellow.

Add half of the cooked rice and fold it into the spiced ghee mixture. Then add the remaining rice and do the same. You are folding the rice in and not stirring harshly or the rice grains will split and become mushy.

If using hot cooked rice, test it for seasoning and serve. If using cold cooked rice from the fridge, continue cooking at 200°C (400°F), lightly stirring from time to time until heated through. Serve garnished with the chopped coriander (cilantro).

# MASALA FRIES

SERVES 2–4

**I'm a big fan of using frozen fries in recipes. Most frozen fries now come with specific air fryer instructions on the packaging, making them easy to follow. If your fries don't include specific guidelines, a good rule of thumb is to set your air fryer to 200°C (400°F) and adjust the cooking time as needed.**

PREP TIME: 5 MINS
COOKING TIME: APPROX.
   15 MINS

350g (12oz) frozen fries
About 2 tbsp rapeseed
   (canola) oil
2 tsp chilli powder
2 green finger or bird's eye
   chillies, thinly sliced
1 tsp ground cumin
1 tsp ground coriander
1 tsp garlic powder
Salt, to taste (optional)

TO FINISH
3 garlic cloves, minced
2–3 green bird's eye chillies,
   finely chopped
1 tbsp chopped coriander
   (cilantro)

Preheat the air fryer to the temperature recommended on the fries packaging. Place the frozen fries in a bowl and coat them evenly with oil. This helps the spices stick to the fries and ensures a crispy texture. Stir in the chilli powder, green chillies, ground cumin, ground coriander and garlic powder. Mix well to ensure each fry is evenly coated with the spice blend.

Arrange the seasoned fries in a single layer in the air fryer basket. Depending on the size of your air fryer, you might need to cook them in batches. Cook for 2 minutes less than the packet instructions.

If you cooked the fries in batches, combine them all in the air fryer basket. Add the fresh garlic and chillies on top. Cook for another 2 minutes to eliminate the rawness of the garlic and chilli, then add the chopped coriander and stir it all in.

Taste one of the fries and add salt to taste. Many brands add salt to their frozen fries, so you may not need to add much or any at all.

Serve the fries hot, topped with the fresh coriander (cilantro). These are good on their own or served with hot sauce, ketchup or any sauce of choice.

NOTE
Some frozen fries are coated with flour to make them extra crispy. If cooking gluten free is important to you, source frozen fries that are wheat flour free.

# BOMBAY POTATOES

SERVES 2–4

**Bombay potatoes make an excellent side dish or main course. Here, you start by air frying the potatoes until crispy on the exterior and soft in the centre. You then prepare an easy but delicious sauce that, when cooked, becomes thick, fragrant and coats the potatoes.**

PREP TIME: 10 MINS
COOKING TIME: 36 MINS

500g (1lb 2oz) floury potatoes, such as Maris Piper or King Edward
Oil spray

FOR THE SAUCE
2 tbsp rapeseed (canola) oil
½ tsp black mustard seeds
½ tsp cumin seeds
½ tsp asafoetida
20 curry leaves
1 red onion, finely chopped
2 green finger chillies, finely chopped
1 tbsp garlic and ginger paste
1 tsp Kashmiri chilli powder (more or less to taste)
½ tsp ground turmeric
½ tsp ground cumin
½ tsp ground coriander
125ml (½ cup) unseasoned passata
Coriander (cilantro), leaves picked, to garnish
Salt and black pepper, to taste

Peel and cut the potatoes into 2.5cm (1in) cubes. Place in a bowl and cover with water for 10 minutes. Before straining, swirl the potatoes around in the water. Strain and pat dry with a paper towel and set aside.

Preheat the air fryer to 200°C (400°F). Spray the cooking basket with oil and place the potatoes inside in one layer. If your cooking basket is not large enough to do this, you will need to cook them in batches, as a good air flow is essential. Spray to coat with oil and air fry for 20 minutes, stirring occasionally for a more even cook. Once the potatoes are crispy and cooked through, transfer them to a plate and set aside.

Pour the oil for the sauce into a metal cake tin or another metal pan that fits into your air fryer. Heat for 2 minutes and then stir in the black mustard seeds to cook for 1 minute or until bubbling hot. Add the cumin seeds, asafoetida and curry leaves and fry for another minute. Then stir in the red onion, chillies, garlic and ginger paste, chilli powder, turmeric, cumin and ground coriander and air fry for a further 3 minutes.

Add the passata, stir well to combine and let it heat up for 5 minutes. Stir in the cooked potatoes and air fry for another 5 minutes or until the potatoes are hot and the sauce is thick and coating them. Season with salt and pepper to taste and garnish with the coriander (cilantro).

# INSTANT NAANS

SERVES 2–4

The dough you use in this recipe is my quick curry house-style one. You could also use the yeast dough featured in my other books, but this one works and gets the job done faster. Want to make these plain naans into garlic versions? Simply air fry about 2 tablespoons of minced garlic in a little ghee at 200°C (400°F) until the ghee is hot and the garlic soft. It should only take a couple of minutes. Then slather it over the top of the hot naans.

PREP TIME: 10 MINS,
PLUS PROVING
COOKING TIME: 10 MINS

125ml (½ cup) warm full-fat (whole) milk
Approx. 110ml (scant ½ cup) water
1 egg, lightly beaten
1 tsp salt
1½ tbsp caster (superfine) sugar
1½ tsp nigella seeds
250g (2 cups) self-raising (self-rising) flour, sifted, plus extra as needed
35ml (⅛ cup) rapeseed (canola) oil
Oil spray
Ghee or melted butter, for brushing (optional)

Pour the milk and water into a large mixing bowl. Add the egg, salt, sugar and nigella seeds and whisk well.

Now start pouring in the flour, whisking as you do. Once you've added all the flour, it will still look very soupy and far too wet to work into dough balls. I recommend covering the dough with a wet cloth and letting it sit for at least 3 hours or overnight for best results. That said, you could just jump right into finishing the recipe at this stage.

When ready to cook your naans, slowly start adding more flour. The idea here is to add just enough flour so that the dough is workable. For reference, I ended up adding about 7 handfuls of flour. It should be very soft and slightly sticky but not so sticky that it sticks to your hands. If it does, dust with a little bit more flour until you can easily divide and form the dough into six spongy dough balls.

Once your dough balls are formed, you could let them sit, covered for about 30 minutes, but again, you could push forward and make your naans immediately.

As the dough is so soft, you shouldn't need a rolling pin. Dip you fingers in the oil and start patting the first dough ball to flatten it. Continue slapping it until it is thin and flat. Repeat with the remaining dough balls. If you roll out your naan dough really thin, you will get crispier naans. Leave them a bit thick and you will have fluffier ones.

Preheat the air fryer to 200°C (400°F). Spray the basket with a little oil and place one or two naans inside. Cook for 3 minutes and then flip your naans over and cook for a further 3 minutes. Note that cooking times may vary depending on the thickness of your naans. The naans need to cook in one layer so you may need to work in batches and keep the cooked naans warm under a clean dish cloth or wrap in foil.

Brush with ghee or melted butter to serve if you like.

# SPICE BLENDS

**Roasting spices is an important step in flavourful spice blends. I have found that using an air fryer to do this is not only much more reliable but also easier than using a pan. Below I have given the ingredients for the spice blends used in this book. The roasting method for each is the same, with the exception of the mixed powder, which uses ground spices so does not need roasting. You just need to roast and grind the whole spices and then add any other ingredients that are called for, such as ground ginger or garlic powder. All of these spice blends are available at Indian shops, some supermarkets and online if you don't want to make your own, but homemade is best.**

## METHOD FOR ROASTING SPICES

Place your whole spices and chillies for your recipe directly into the drawer of your air fryer. It is essential that they be in one layer and not piled up. Preheat the air fryer to 180°C (350°F). Cover with the basket, which will stop the spices from blowing around in the drawer as they roast, for 3–5 minutes, shaking one or two times for more even cooking. The spices are ready when warm to the touch and fragrant. You should be able to smell them when they are almost ready.

Allow to cool and then blend to a fine powder in a spice grinder or pestle and mortar. If additional ground spices are called for, stir them in. These spice blends are best used on the day you make them but will keep in an airtight container for up to 3 months.

## GARAM MASALA

MAKES APPROX. 6 TBSP

2 tbsp coriander seeds
2 tbsp cumin seeds
2 tsp black peppercorns
1 tsp fennel seeds
1 tsp cloves
2.5cm (1in) cinnamon stick
2 dried Indian bay leaves (cassia leaves – optional)
7 green cardamom pods, lightly crushed
1 small blade mace

## MIXED POWDER

MAKES GENEROUS 5 TBSP

**There is no need to roast these spices.**

1 tbsp ground cumin
1 tbsp ground ginger
1½ tbsp Madras curry powder
1 tbsp paprika
1 tbsp ground turmeric
1 tsp garam masala

## TANDOORI MASALA

**MAKES APPROX. 4 TBSP**

1 tbsp coriander seeds
1 tbsp cumin seeds
1 tsp black mustard seeds
2.5cm (1in) cinnamon stick
1 Indian bay leaf (cassia leaf – optional)
1 tsp ground ginger
2 tsp garlic powder
2 tsp onion powder
2 tsp amchoor (dried mango powder)
1 tsp red food colouring powder (optional)

## MADRAS CURRY POWDER

**MAKES APPROX. 9 TBSP**

2 tbsp coriander seeds
2 tbsp cumin seeds
2 tsp fennel seeds
2 tsp black mustard seeds
4cm (1½in) cinnamon stick
1 Indian bay leaf (cassia leaf – optional)
1 tbsp fenugreek seeds
1 star anise
5 cardamom pods, lightly crushed
3–5 dried Kashmiri chillies
2 tsp ground turmeric
2 tsp hot chilli powder (optional and more or less
    to taste)
1 tsp garlic powder
1 tsp onion powder

## CHAAT MASALA

**MAKES GENEROUS 4 TBSP**

1 tbsp cumin seeds
1 tbsp coriander seeds
½ tsp Kashmiri chilli powder
1½ tsp amchoor (dried mango powder)
1 tbsp black salt
A pinch asafoetida
1 tsp dried mint leaves (optional)
1 tsp ground ginger
¼ tsp ajwain (carom) seeds

## MEAT MASALA

**MAKES APPROX. 6 TBSP**

4 tbsp coriander seeds
2 tbsp cumin seeds
½ tsp black (royal) cumin
½ tsp fenugreek seeds
1 tbsp black peppercorns
1 tbsp fennel seeds
1 tsp cloves
2.5cm (1in) cinnamon stick
4 dried red bird's eye chillies
4 dried Kashmiri red chillies
Seeds from 5 green cardamom pods
Seeds from 2 black cardamom pods
1 star anise
1 blade mace
1 tsp citric acid powder

# GARLIC, GINGER AND CHILLI PASTE

MAKES APPROX. 15 TBSP

You will need garlic and ginger paste for most of the recipes in this book. It is easy to prepare and also freezes well. I recommend freezing it in ice-cube trays in 1–2 tablespoon portions and then storing the cubes in freezer bags. I usually make the garlic and ginger paste and then blend chillies to taste into it to make garlic, ginger and chilli paste. You could also just blend the chillies on their own as they freeze well too. Then just mix the garlic and ginger paste and chilli pastes as required.

PREP TIME: 10 MINS

150g (5½oz) garlic, roughly chopped
150g (5½oz) ginger, roughly chopped
Green finger chillies, to taste

For garlic and ginger paste, blend the garlic and ginger with just enough water to make a paste. This will keep in the fridge for up to 5 days. It might turn a bit blue or green in the fridge but this is normal. It's not off! Blend and add green finger chillies as required.

# FRIED ONIONS

SERVES 2–4

Crispy fried onions have many uses. They can be used as a garnish or added to a curry to both flavour and thicken the sauce. These air fryer fried onions are better than shop-bought versions and are perfect for use in the biryani recipe on page 64.

PREP TIME: 5 MINS
COOKING TIME: APPROX. 30 MINS

2 large onions, thinly sliced
2 tbsp ghee or oil spray

Place the sliced onions in a bowl and either add the ghee or spray to coat with oil spray. Mix well. Set your air fryer to 200°C (400°F) and place the sliced onions in the basket. Cook for 5 minutes and then stir well. Cook for another 5 minutes and stir again. At this point, your onions will be beginning to darken in places. Stir well again and cook for another 5 minutes.

Now reduce the temperature to 150°C/300°F and continue cooking, stirring every 2–3 minutes, until the onions are a deep golden brown and crispy. This could take another 15 minutes.

Use the fried onions in biryanis (see page 64) or stir them into a curry even if not called for in the recipe. They will most definitely add a nice flavour. Although you can store the onions for a week or more in an airtight container, I recommend just making the amount you need.

# EASY TAMARIND CHUTNEY
SERVES 4

**This easy tamarind chutney is delicious served with the Aloo tikki chaat on page 17. It is also nice as a dipping sauce for poppadums.**

PREP TIME: 5 MINS, PLUS SITTING TIME

1–2 tbsp tamarind concentrate
2 tbsp water
3 tbsp sugar
4 tbsp tomato ketchup
Juice of 1 lemon
3 green chillies, finely chopped
½ onion, finely chopped
3 spring onions (scallions), finely chopped
4 tbsp finely chopped coriander (cilantro)
1 large carrot, grated (optional)
1 tsp curry powder
Salt, to taste

Put all the ingredients into a small bowl and mix well. Refrigerate for at least 1 hour before serving. Leftovers can be stored in an airtight container or covered tightly in the fridge for up to 3 days.

# CORIANDER, MINT AND MANGO CHUTNEY
SERVES 4

**This is a quick, easy and very delicious chutney that is great served slathered over kebabs or as a dipping sauce. It is also amazing with the Aloo tikki chaat on page 17.**

PREP TIME: 5 MINS

Small bunch of coriander (cilantro), leaves only
Large bunch of mint, leaves only
200ml (generous ¾ cup) smooth mango chutney
1–4 fresh green chillies, to taste, finely chopped
2 garlic cloves, finely chopped
Juice of 1 lime
Salt, to taste

Roughly chop the coriander (cilantro) and mint leaves and place in a blender with the remaining ingredients, seasoning with salt. Blend until smooth. Taste and look at it. If you would like a thicker sauce, add more coriander or mint, or for a sweeter sauce; just add more mango chutney, or add lime juice for a tarter flavour. Store covered in the fridge and use within 3 days.

# TARKA DAL

SERVES 2–4

**There are some things that are just plain better cooked using more traditional methods and I'm afraid dal is one of them. I decided to include this recipe when my daughter returned home from university, found my air fried tarka dal in the fridge, heated it up in the microwave and gobbled it all up. She had no idea the dal had been air fried! This may not be the best way to cook a tarka dal but it works at a pinch and might come in handy for you one day. The dal is used in the chicken dhansak on page 61. This recipe only works for masoor dal (red lentils) and I recommend soaking the lentils in water overnight if you have time.**

PREP TIME: 15 MINS,
PLUS SOAKING
COOKING TIME: 45 MINS

1 cup masoor lentils, rinsed and soaked in water for 30–60 minutes or longer, then drained
500ml (2 cups) boiling water
Salt, to taste

FOR THE TEMPERING
4 tbsp rapeseed (canola) oil or ghee
1 tbsp cumin seeds
1 onion, finely chopped
2 medium tomatoes, diced
1 tbsp ground cumin
1 tbsp ground coriander
½ tsp ground turmeric
1 tbsp roughly chopped garlic
1 tbsp finely chopped ginger
2 green bird's eye chillies

Place the soaked and strained masoor lentils in a small cake tin or another metal pan that fits into your air fryer basket. Cover with the boiling water. You can heat the water in a kettle for ease. Preheat the air fryer to 200°C (400°F) and air fry for 40 minutes, stirring often. Once the lentils are soft, mash them with a potato masher. There is no need to strain and you might even want to add a little boiling water for a creamier texture. Season with salt to taste, cover and keep warm.

Once again, preheat the air fryer to 200°C (400°F). Pour the oil into a metal cake tin or another metal pan that fits into your air fryer and heat it for 3 minutes. Stir in the cumin and onion and air fry for 5 minutes, stirring every minute to check that it isn't burning and to cook the onion evenly.

Stir in the chopped tomatoes and ground spices and fry for another 4–6 minutes, stirring every 2 minutes. Add the garlic, ginger and whole chillies and air fry for another 2 minutes. Pour this tarka over the cooked lentils and serve immediately.

# INDEX

## A

achari, lamb 70
air fryer base sauce 38
air fryers, using as a
    tandoor oven 89
aloo gobi 85
aloo tikki chaat 17

## B

base sauce, air fryer 38
basics
    coriander, mint and mango
        chutney 121
    easy tamarind chutney 121
    fried onions 120
    garlic, ginger and chilli paste
        120
    spice blends 118–19
    tarka dal 122
basmati rice
    fried pilau rice 111
    perfect air fryer basmati rice
        110
beef
    beef bhuna 75
    beef chapli kebabs 28
    cheese-filled koftas with
        chilli raita 101
    keema 72
    meat tikka with cucumber
        raita 93
    nargisi koftas 34
beef marrow: beef chapli
    kebabs 28
beef tikka 93
    beef bhuna 75
bhajis, onion 18
bhuna, beef 75
biryani, chicken 64
blenders 10
Bombay potatoes 114
breads: instant naans 117
butter paneer 83

## C

cake tin inserts 10
cashews

chicken Ceylon 55
chicken korma 42
cauliflower: aloo gobi 85
chaat masala 119
    chicken chaat 62
chapli kebabs, beef 28
chasni, chicken 47
cheese
    butter paneer 83
    cheese-filled koftas with chilli
        raita 101
    hariyali paneer and vegetable
        skewers 33
    paneer papad rolls 30
    saag paneer 80
    stuffed mushrooms 106
chef's knife 10
chicken
    chicken biryani 64
    chicken Ceylon 55
    chicken chaat 62
    chicken chasni 47
    chicken chilli garlic 51
    chicken dhansak 61
    chicken jalfrezi 45
    chicken korma 42
    chicken methi 59
    chicken pasanda 56
    chicken pathia 52
    chicken rezala 48
    chicken 65 20
    chicken tikka 90
    chicken tikka masala 40
    easy whole tandoori
        chicken 94
    quick tandoori chicken legs 24
    southern-style tandoori
        chicken 97
chickpeas: chicken chaat 62
chilli raita 101
    aloo tikki chaat 17
chillies
    chicken chilli garlic 51
    chicken jalfrezi 45
    chilli raita 101
    garlic, ginger and chilli
        paste 120
    hariyali paneer and vegetable
        skewers 33
    lamb achari 70
    lamb andrak 77
    masala fries 112

onion chutney 14
paneer papad rolls 30
tandoori prawns 103
chutney
    coriander chutney 99
    coriander, mint and mango
        chutney 121
    easy tamarind chutney 121
    onion chutney 14
coconut milk
    chicken Ceylon 55
    chicken korma 42
    chicken pasanda 56
    southern-style tandoori
        chicken 97
cooking temperatures 10, 37
cooking times 10
coriander (cilantro)
    aloo tikki chaat 17
    coriander chutney 99
    coriander, mint and mango
        chutney 121
    cucumber raita 93
    easy tamarind chutney 121
cream cheese: stuffed
    mushrooms 106
cucumber raita 93
curries 36–87
    air fryer base sauce 38
    aloo gobi 85
    beef bhuna 75
    butter paneer 83
    chicken biryani 64
    chicken Ceylon 55
    chicken chaat 62
    chicken chasni 47
    chicken chilli garlic 51
    chicken dhansak 61
    chicken jalfrezi 45
    chicken korma 42
    chicken methi 59
    chicken pasanda 56
    chicken pathia 52
    chicken rezala 48
    chicken tikka masala 40
    keema 72
    lamb achari 70
    lamb andrak 77
    lamb dopiaza 67
    lamb madras 78
    lamb rogan josh 69
    rajma 86

saag paneer 80
curry leaves
    Bombay potatoes 114
    chicken Ceylon 55
    chicken 65 20
    southern-style tandoori
        chicken 97
    stuffed mushrooms 106

### D
dal, tarka 122
dhansak, chicken 61
dopiaza, lamb 67
dunghar smoking method 89

### E
eggs: nargisi koftas 34
equipment 10

### F
fish
    Lahori fish tikka 26
    tandoori sea bream 104
flatbreads: instant naans 117
fries, masala 112

### G
garam masala 118
garlic
    chicken chilli garlic 51
    chicken 65 20
    cucumber raita 93
    garlic, ginger and chilli paste
        120
garlic, ginger and chilli paste 120
    southern-style tandoori
        chicken 97
    tandoori lamb chops with
        coriander chutney 99
ginger
    garlic, ginger and chilli paste
        120
    lamb andrak 77

### H
hariyali paneer and vegetable
    skewers 33

### I
ingredients 37

### J
jalfrezi, chicken 45

### K
kebabs
    beef chapli kebabs 28
    lamb seekh kebabs 23
keema 72
ketchup
    easy tamarind chutney 121
    pakora sauce 18
kettles 10
kidney beans: rajma 86
knives, chef's 10
koftas
    cheese-filled koftas with chilli
        raita 101
    nargisi koftas 34
korma, chicken 42

### L
Lahori fish tikka 26
lamb
    cheese-filled koftas with chilli
        raita 101
    keema 72
    lamb achari 70
    lamb andrak 77
    lamb dopiaza 67
    lamb madras 78
    lamb rogan josh 69
    lamb seekh kebabs 23
    meat tikka 93
    nargisi koftas 34
    tandoori lamb chops with
        coriander chutney 99
lamb tikka 93
    lamb achari 70
    lamb andrak 77
    lamb dopiaza 67
    lamb rogan josh 69
lemons: chicken tikka 90
lentils
    chicken dhansak 61
    tarka dal 122

### M
madras
    lamb madras 78

madras curry powder 119
mango chutney
    coriander, mint and mango
        chutney 121
    pakora sauce 18
    paneer papad rolls 30
masala
    chaat masala 119
    garam masala 118
    masala fries 112
    meat masala 119
    tandoori masala 119
masoor dal
    chicken dhansak 61
    tarka dal 122
meat
    meat masala 119
    meat tikka with cucumber
        raita 93
    see also beef; chicken; lamb
meat thermometer 10
methi (fenugreek leaves):
        chicken methi 59
mint
    coriander, mint and mango
        chutney 121
    paneer papad rolls 30
mushrooms, stuffed 106
mustard greens: saag paneer 80

### N
naans, instant 117
nargisi koftas 34

### O
oil 9
onions
    air fryer base sauce 38
    fried onions 120
    lamb dopiaza 67
    onion bhajis with pakora
        sauce 18
    onion chutney 14

### P
pakora sauce 18
panch poran: lamb achari 70
paneer
    butter paneer 83
    hariyali paneer and vegetable
        skewers 33

paneer papad rolls 30
saag paneer 80
stuffed mushrooms 106
panko breadcrumbs
  nargisi koftas 34
  stuffed mushrooms 106
pans 10
papads
  paneer papad rolls 30
  poppadums with onion
    chutney 14
pasanda, chicken 56
pathia, chicken 52
peppers
  aloo gobi 85
  beef bhuna 75
  butter paneer 83
  chicken dhansak 61
  lamb dopiaza 67
  lamb madras 78
  lamb rogan josh 69
  rajma 86
pilau rice, fried 111
pineapple: chicken dhansak 61
pineapple juice: chicken
  dhansak 61
poppadums with onion
  chutney 14
potatoes
  aloo gobi 85
  aloo tikki chaat 17
  Bombay potatoes 114
prawns, tandoori 103

R

raita
  chilli raita 101
  cucumber raita 93
rajma 86
rezala, chicken 48
rice
  chicken biryani 64
  fried pilau rice 111
  perfect air fryer basmati
    rice 110
rogan josh, lamb 69

S

saag paneer 80
scaling up recipes 9–10

sea bream, tandoori 104
seekh kebabs, lamb 23
side dishes 108–117
  Bombay potatoes 114
  fried pilau rice 111
  instant naans 117
  masala fries 112
  perfect air fryer basmati
    rice 110
skewers, hariyali paneer and
  vegetable 33
smoking methods: dunghar
  method 89
snacks and starters see starters
  and snacks
southern-style tandoori chicken
  97
spice blends 118–19
  chaat masala 119
  garam masala 118
  madras curry powder 119
  meat masala 119
  mixed powder 118
  tandoori masala 119
spice dabba 10
spices, roasting 118
spinach: saag paneer 80
starters and snacks 12–35
  aloo tikki chaat 17
  beef chapli kebabs 28
  chicken 65 20
  hariyali paneer and vegetable
    skewers 33
  Lahori fish tikka 26
  lamb seekh kebabs 23
  nargisi koftas 34
  onion bhajis with pakora sauce
    18
  paneer papad rolls 30
  poppadums with onion
    chutney 14
  quick tandoori chicken legs 24
stick blender 10
stuffed mushrooms 106

T

tamarind chutney 121
  aloo tikki chaat 17
tandoori 88–107
  cheese-filled koftas with chilli

    raita 101
  chicken tikka 90
  easy whole tandoori
    chicken 94
  meat tikka with cucumber
    raita 93
  southern-style tandoori
    chicken 97
  tandoori chicken legs 24
  tandoori lamb chops with
    coriander chutney 99
  tandoori masala 119
  tandoori prawns 103
  tandoori sea bream 104
tarka dal 122
thermometer, meat 10
tikka
  chicken tikka 90
  Lahori fish tikka 26
  meat tikka with cucumber
    raita 93
tikka masala, chicken 40
tomatoes
  aloo gobi 85
  beef chapli kebabs 28
  butter paneer 83
  chicken biryani 64
  lamb madras 78
  lamb rogan josh 69
  rajma 86
  tandoori prawns 103

V

vegetables
  hariyali paneer and vegetable
    skewers 33
  see also individual types of
    vegetable

Y

yoghurt
  chicken biryani 64
  chicken tikka 90
  chilli raita 101
  cucumber raita 93
  pakora sauce 18
  quick tandoori chicken legs 24
  southern-style tandoori
    chicken 97

# ACKNOWLEDGEMENTS

It was a pleasure to once again work with everyone at Quadrille to produce this book. Thank you to Sarah Lavelle for commissioning the project and to my editors, Vicky Orchard and Sofie Shearman, for all their help with my words and for bringing it all together.

Thanks to Kris Kirkham, who has worked with me on every cookbook I've written, and food stylists Rosie Reynolds and Troy Willis for bringing my recipes to life in a way that only they can. Thank you also to Kris's assistant, Yelena Aleksić and food stylist assistant Jess Geddes. We could not have done it without them!

Thank you to props stylist Faye Wears, who sourced the props and dishes. They were perfect!

A big thank you goes out to the moderators of my Facebook group: Jon Monday, Steven Lumsden, Tim Martin, Karen Bolan, Claire Rees, Anne-Marie Goodfellow, James Vaisey. Your help and support is so much appreciated.

Thank you to my agent, Clare Hulton, for all her support and for once again making things happen.

I could not have written this book without my wife Caroline's support. She helped cook every recipe to ensure that the recipes worked and tasted as they should.

I would also like to thank my son Joe Toombs and his fiancé, Shannon Ellerton, for their help with the recipes. They cooked and tested most, if not all, of these recipes and filmed many of them being made for my blog and social media. Their feedback and help perfecting these recipes for the home cook has been invaluable. They read and prepared each recipe as written, sometimes catching problems I didn't want going in a printed book. Thank you!

One last big thank you, and that goes out to you for picking up this book. I appreciate it so much and hope you enjoy the book and recipes as much as I enjoyed putting this collection together.

Managing Director: Sarah Lavelle
Project Editors: Vicky Orchard and
Sofie Shearman
Designer: Alicia House
Cover Design: Smith & Gilmour
Photographer: Kris Kirkham
Photography Assistant: Yelena Aleksić
Food Stylists: Rosie Reynolds and Troy Willis
Food Stylist Assistants: Jessica Geddes
Props Stylist: Faye Wears
Head of Production: Stephen Lang
Production Manager: Sabeena Atchia

Colour reproduction by F1
Printed in China by C&C Offset Printing Co., Ltd.

The authorised representative in the EEA is
Penguin Random House Ireland, Morrison
Chambers, 32 Nassau Street, Dublin D02
YH68.

Penguin Random House is committed to a
sustainable future for our business, our
readers and our planet. This book is made
from Forest Stewardship Council® certified
paper.

Quadrille, Penguin Random House UK, One
Embassy Gardens, 8 Viaduct Gardens,
London SW11 7BW

Quadrille Publishing Limited is part of the
Penguin Random House group of companies
whose addresses can be found at global.
penguinrandomhouse.com

Penguin
Random House
UK

Published by Quadrille in 2025

www.penguin.co.uk
A CIP catalogue record for this book is
available from the British Library

ISBN 978 183 783 317 7
10 9 8 7 6 5 4 3 2 1

In five short years Dan took The Curry Guy from an idea to a reliable brand. The recipes are all developed and tested in Dan's home kitchen. And they work. His bestselling cookbooks and the 750,000 curry fans who visit his blog www.greatcurryrecipes.net every month can testify to that fact. This is Dan's 10th cookbook.

If you have any recipe questions, you can contact Dan (@thecurryguy) on X, Facebook or Instagram.